If you have a home computer with Internet access you may:
- request an item to be placed on hold.
- renew an item that is not overdue or on hold.
- view titles and due dates checked out on your card.
- view and/or pay your outstanding fines online ($1 & over).

To view your patron record from your home computer click on Patchogue-Medford Library's homepage: www.pmlib.org

Ethics without Morals

Routledge Studies in Ethics and Moral Theory

1 **The Contradictions of Modern Moral Philosophy**
Ethics after Wittgenstein
Paul Johnston

2 **Kant, Duty and Moral Worth**
Philip Stratton-Lake

3 **Justifying Emotions**
Pride and Jealousy
Kristján Kristjánsson

4 **Classical Utilitarianism from Hume to Mill**
Frederick Rosen

5 **The Self, the Soul and the Psychology of Good and Evil**
Ilham Dilman

6 **Moral Responsibility**
The Ways of Scepticism
Carlos J. Moya

7 **The Ethics of Confucius and Aristotle**
Mirrors of Virtue
Jiyuan Yu

8 **Caste Wars**
A Philosophy of Discrimination
David Edmonds

9 **Deprivation and Freedom**
A Philosophical Enquiry
Richard J. Hull

10 **Needs and Moral Necessity**
Soran Reader

11 **Reasons, Patterns, and Cooperation**
Christopher Woodard

12 **Challenging Moral Particularism**
Edited by *Mark Norris Lance, Matjaž Potrč, and Vojko Strahovnik*

13 **Rationality and Moral Theory**
How Intimacy Generates Reasons
Diane Jeske

14 **The Ethics of Forgiveness**
A Collection of Essays
Christel Fricke

15 **Moral Exemplars in the Analects**
The Good Person is That
Amy Olberding

16 **The Phenomenology of Moral Normativity**
William H. Smith

17 **The Second-Person Perspective in Aquinas's Ethics**
Virtues and Gifts
Andrew Pinsent

18 **Social Humanism**
A New Metaphysics
Brian Ellis

19 **Ethics without Morals**
In Defense of Amorality
Joel Marks

Ethics without Morals
In Defense of Amorality

Joel Marks

Routledge
Taylor & Francis Group
NEW YORK LONDON

First published 2013
by Routledge
711 Third Avenue, New York, NY 10017

Simultaneously published in the UK
by Routledge
2 Park Square, Milton Park, Abingdon, Oxon OX14 4RN

*Routledge is an imprint of the Taylor & Francis Group,
an informa business*

© 2013 Taylor & Francis

The right of Joel Marks to be identified as author of this work has been asserted by him in accordance with sections 77 and 78 of the Copyright, Designs and Patents Act 1988.

All rights reserved. No part of this book may be reprinted or reproduced or utilised in any form or by any electronic, mechanical, or other means, now known or hereafter invented, including photocopying and recording, or in any information storage or retrieval system, without permission in writing from the publishers.

Trademark Notice: Product or corporate names may be trademarks or registered trademarks, and are used only for identification and explanation without intent to infringe.

Library of Congress Cataloging-in-Publication Data
Marks, Joel, 1949–
  Ethics without morals : in defence of amorality / by Joel Marks.
    p. cm. -- (Routledge studies in ethics and moral theory ; 19)
  Includes bibliographical references (p.) and index.
  1. Ethics. I. Title.
  BJ1031.M3153 2012
  170—dc23
                                2012020547

ISBN: 978-0-415-63556-1 (hbk)
ISBN: 978-0-203-09307-8 (ebk)

Typeset in Sabon
by IBT Global.

Printed and bound in the United States of America on sustainably sourced paper by IBT Global.

To Jack Davis, Jerry Shaffer, and Joel Kupperman, my steadfast mentors from graduate school to retirement (mine!) and beyond.

Contents

	Acknowledgments	ix
	Introduction	1
1	What Is Morality?	4
2	Does Morality Exist?	16
3	Would Amorality Be Viable?	26
4	Might Amorality Be Preferable?	35
5	Is Amorality Just Another Way of Being Moral?	56
6	How Shall We Treat Other Animals? A Case Study in Applied Amorality	67
7	What Is Ethics?	82
	Notes	95
	Bibliography	123
	Index	129

Acknowledgments

How this book came to be is a story in itself, which in fact I have told (in part) in a memoir which preceded it. This has been a personal journey as well as a professional one, and in both respects, many other individuals have been integral to it. Therefore I will combine a brief recapitulation of what transpired with acknowledgments to many friends and colleagues.

As with any series of events, there have been some noteworthy coincidences. One is that the episode that precipitated all that has followed occurred on Christmas Day (of 2007). I call this a coincidence because I think on that day I heard the glad tidings of the end of moral guilt, which is the secular equivalent of sin. Another coincidence is that the episode took place in the home of Mitchell Silver, whose ideas in his 2006 book, *A Plausible God*, have contributed both causally and substantively to the central argument of the present book. I call this a coincidence because Mitchell was not even present, nor his ideas in mind, when the episode took place.

The person who was present along with me was H____, with whom I was having a conversation about God. This was not unusual for us, as H____ is a minister and I was an agnostic. But there is still more of coincidence, or perhaps now it tends to irony. For it was discussion with H____ that had inspired my previous monograph, which was a defense of morality; whereas the result of the later discussion was to be my "counter-conversion" to amorality.

(It was also ironic—or maybe absurd, or simply funny—that the thoughts that came to me from that conversation were apparently due to my misunderstanding what H____ was telling me . . . as she later explained to me . . . I think! None of this bothers me in the least, as it fits quite well with my new view of life as largely governed by unseen causes. But I had already become sympathetic to the manner of accidental inspiration from hearing Sam Wheeler in a seminar when I was in graduate school wax breezily about his own inspiration for a particular thesis from having possibly misunderstood the ancient Greeks.)

What then happened during that epochal conversation? Without filling in the narrative, I will only say that I realized that morality is like God. This had a double effect on me. It made me more receptive to theism, as committing one to something less consequential than I had previously supposed; and this was a good thing for me to realize, I felt, because I could then be in better accord with H____. But it also produced a panic and disappointment in me as I suddenly saw morality in the same light, as also less consequential than I had previously supposed. For about morality I had never been agnostic but always a true believer.

Over the course of a year or two this original insight evolved and transformed. At first my world still contained both God and morality; it was only that their natures had changed. Specifically, they were both simply an interaction between some non-supernatural reality external to the individual and the emotional response of the individual. God was the universe responded to with awe; right and wrong were human actions responded to with approval or disapproval. But this implied that most theists and moralists were making a mistake, namely, to believe that God was a self-existing supernatural entity and right and wrong were objective properties of human actions, respectively.

I found cause for both elation and despair in this new view of things, in particular, of morality. On the one hand, many mysteries were solved or dissolved. For example, as a staunch moralist I had been perplexed by the seeming impossibility of proving things I took to be indubitable moral truths—from the trivial (It is wrong for my neighbor to play his stereo so loud) to the world-shaking (It is wrong to fly an airliner into a skyscraper). I remember watching the televised scenes of angry hordes overseas who cheered at the destruction of the World Trade Center towers and wondering how there could be millions who were so evil or at least so mistaken. Little did I know that that wondering would evolve into doubt and eventually bear fruit analogously to the child wondering how Santa Claus could reach every household in a single night. Now, as a result of my Christmas Day revelation, all was made plain: Morality is *essentially* relative.

But of course this was also shocking to me. If my own moral take on things is merely my psychological response to events, then it would seem to lose its defining authority as moral. It is one thing to like chocolate ice cream and quite another to, say, condemn theft, one would have thought. We tend to react quite differently to someone else's disliking the flavor we like and to someone's stealing our wallet. And the difference is supposed to be not only that we have a stronger desire to retain our wallet than to have our favorite flavor universally endorsed; it's that liking chocolate ice cream is only a matter of taste, whereas the wrongness of stealing is a matter of fact. But now that latter distinction had vanished from my mind. The only facts in either case were matters of subjective preference: The owner would prefer to keep his wallet and the thief would prefer to abscond with it. That's it. So how could I condemn the thief? Indeed, why not become a thief myself?

These questions were not merely theoretical for me. I had no particular inclination to become a thief, but I had, at around the same time as this upheaval of thought, as it happened, become preoccupied with animal ethics. It was a profound revelation to me that the way so-called food animals are now bred and raised and slaughtered in industrial agriculture is an evil unsurpassed in human history. But no sooner had I been filled with this conviction than the moral rug was pulled out from under my feet. Perplexity seems too tame a word to describe the puzzlement and distress I thereupon experienced.

It did not take long for me to draw the further conclusion that a relative morality is tantamount to no morality at all, given the conception of morality I had held. Thus, I began to speak of "amorality." (This also had the side effect of transforming both my original agnosticism and subsequent interactionist theism into an out-and-out atheism. I thence conceived the project of convincing the so-called new atheists that their work would not be complete until they had dispelled the belief in morality as well.) This led to anxious feelings of another kind: I seemed to myself like someone who should skulk in alleyways. It was not so much a sense of guilt (which would be a contradiction for an amoralist) as a genuine fear of how I would be looked upon by the rest of society. I honestly—although as it turned out, naïvely—thought my new point of view would be a shock and a scandal to the world at large.

While all this was happening I began to write about it. I felt the desperate need to figure out everything—life, my life—from scratch. As my philosophical memoir grew in length, I began to see the benefits of this new way of conceiving human action and character. Finally I reached a point where I felt that, far from needing to hide my amorality from the world, I should share it with the world. It would be a gift. At the very least, it was important—perhaps the most important thing in the world! I also saw the humor in my situation; it was not lost on me that I was becoming an unbelieving proselytizer. Nevertheless, this did not dissuade me from the conviction that I had stumbled upon a truth of epic proportions. I wrote a semiserious little essay expressing annoyance that my discovery would, however, never appear on the front page of *The New York Times*, whereas something as abstruse as Wiles' (purportedly) proving Fermat's last theorem did. One of the most amazing and amusing parts of this story is that it *did*, apparently, end up on the front page of *The New York Times*—of the online edition, that is, with the publication of my Opinionator columns on the subject.

Meanwhile, amidst the throes of writing my way out of my existential predicament, I recalled to mind various books and authors I had some vague knowledge of, and I set about to read (or reread) them. These naturally led me to other books, as did various friends and colleagues to whom I was opening up. I began to realize that I was not alone. But it was not until I had finished writing the manuscript of *Bad Faith: A Philosophical Memoir* that I delved into the literature in earnest. The delay had two causes: I was caught up in thinking everything through for myself, and it never dawned on me that something so novel in my own experience could already have been explored extensively in a recognized corpus. A layperson reading this account probably does not realize that the field of philosophy, like so many other disciplines, is replete with subspecialties. I could only claim to have had real competence in so-called normative ethics, which includes the study of moral theories; and in particular I had focused on the issue known as consequentialism.

Thus it was possible for me to have the merest acquaintance with another branch of ethics known as meta-ethics, under which rubric the philosophical content of the present volume would be considered to fall. I will not belabor you with the technical niceties, other than to say that the position (or actually two positions) I defend herein has been variously called moral skepticism, moral antirealism, moral error theory, moral nihilism, moral eliminativism, and moral abolitionism in the contemporary literature of meta-ethics. As I say, I did not become really familiar with that literature, or even know of its existence as a genre, until after I had written my memoir. But while that was not my plan, I am thankful for that sequence; had I arrived at amorality as a result of reading rather than revelation and writing, I doubt I would understand it as well as I do. Again, this was not a scholarly or academic project for me at the beginning; it was an urgent existential search for a way to live in light of a devastating discovery.

Bad Faith, almost twice the length of the present monograph, remains unpublished. I recognized after multiple rejections from publishers that it is a mishmash of autobiography and treatise. Hence I set out to write *Ethics without Morals* as a "pure" monograph, knowing it would find an academic publisher. (At some future date I may try to rescue the remainder as a "pure" memoir.) The present work is therefore a dotting of the i's and crossing of the t's—but an exercise not to be despised for all that. I think of the analogy of studying English in school. Even though we enter school speaking our native tongue and so understanding it implicitly in a very deep sense, we certainly also benefit a great deal from its formal study.

But for me the real joy has been to discover so many confirming "testimonies" in the literature, and even to strike up several collegial friendships with both challengers and sympathizers. I must however single out Richard Garner, who is my true soul mate in this matter. His concurrence and encouragement—indeed, his very existence has been a comfort, for otherwise I would have felt much more alone in my convictions. But I knew nothing of Richard or his 1994 book, *Beyond Morality*, until my memoir was completed. When I did discover them, quite by accident, I was delighted but also subject to some trepidation lest *Bad Faith*, should it be published, seem a work of blatant plagiarism. (This experience was to be repeated with several other authors, particularly when reading the work of Richard Joyce ... not to mention Nietzsche!) When finally putting my own thoughts into a vehicle—the present monograph—that has been fully informed by the relevant professional literature, I was blessed to receive Richard Garner's meticulous, erudite, and well-wishing criticism every word of the way.

Acknowledgments xiii

At the same time, Richard has been honing to perfection his own book for a second edition, with ample admiring and critical commentary from me in return. Neither of us has any fear of tramping on the other's toes. Our styles are quite different, we each have some original arguments, and we even have some substantive differences (although not regarding the core). Perhaps our main divergence is that I see moral thinking and attitudes as more pervasive than does Richard. For example, Richard fancies himself free still to be angry about many things, whereas I now view all anger as indignation, which is an inherently moral emotion; so I seek to banish it from the world, including from my own soul. Richard is not a fan of anger but he is comfortable inside his own occasionally irritated skin. I envy him. He denies it, but he is a Zen master. I seem fated to be an aspiring saint.

Meanwhile, Mitchell Silver has taken a very special interest in my amoralism project from its inception. Mitchell had been my constant interlocutor since we met in our graduate philosophy program at the University of Connecticut 36 years ago, but never before had he been quite so enthusiastic about one of my philosophical explorations as he became about this one. He seems to have been seized by its effect on me even more than by my thesis and arguments. In fact he either rejects the thesis or else holds it to be existential and hence beyond argument (and so in that sense it is not even a thesis). He was even pressing me to transform my original memoir—about which he filled a notebook with 40 pages of handwritten commentary!—into a novel in the *Notes from Underground* genre. (Alas, lacking that particular type of writing facility, I have gone to the opposite extreme and turned it into the treatise before you, which addresses many of Mitchell's earlier concerns and a draft of which he subsequently reviewed as well.)

Besides being a bottomless resource, sharp (but blunt!) critic, and steadfast booster all these years, Mitchell has provided me with two key insights for the present venture. One is this (in my words from Chapter 5): "Even if there were a plausible conception of morality that escaped my existential attack on its having omitted an allegedly essential element, I would argue that the connotative echo of the missing element would cause so much mischief that we would still want to dispense with moral language." Mitchell had made an analogous claim in his book about God and theistic language. Curiously, however, he does not accept my appropriation of it for the critique of morality. Mitchell maintains that morality serves a far more essential role in human affairs than (belief in) God and sees no reason to dispense with it. This despite the fact that he and I agree there is no such thing as what I call metaphysical morality. But Mitchell does not thereby go the route of Richard Joyce in embracing a moral fictionalism; instead, in the book on which he is currently working, Mitchell defends a different conception of morality, such that it manifestly exists in reality.

The other insight I owe to Mitchell came in an email from him: "It seems easy to imagine how evolution could equip us with logically inconsistent intuitions if, in most lives, it was useful to have them both." That email was sent to me on January 5, 2008—less than two weeks after the Christmas Day on which the scales had begun to fall from my eyes. I had already started writing *Bad Faith* (on New Year's Day), so I must by then have been in heated dialogue with Mitchell about the new idea. I think I can safely say, however, that the date of the email is when the idea crystallized. (I cite as circumstantial evidence my having scrawled on my calendar for that day, "<u>Everything</u> falls into place.") Yet I see now that the way had also been paved by a remark, uttered almost as an aside, made by another fast friend and interlocutor, Wendell Wallach, at a colloquium I gave on animal ethics at a meeting of the Hartford Ethics Group at Trinity College (to which I had been invited by the coordinator, Halley Faust). That meeting (at which, by another coincidence, H____ had also been present) took place the month *before* my fateful discussion with H____ in Mitchell's home.

Wendell's comment was to the effect that moral theories are first and foremost intuitions. This, in retrospect, was the true ground-shaking of my moralist foundations. (It is hardly news to meta-ethicists, but, recall, I had not been intimately acquainted with that literature. To me it was a revelation—marvelous and terrifying at the same time.) Mitchell's comment having brought it to fruition in my consciousness, I initiated a dialogue about it with Wendell as well. Am I not blessed to have such friends and colleagues?

Other contemporary influences on the present project include Joshua Greene's (2007) demotion of Kantianism, Jesse Prinz's (2007) promotion of emotions, David Wong's (2006) functionalist grounding of moral relativism, and Daniel Dennett's (1966) explication of Darwinism as well as his (2006) Darwinian analysis of theism. In addition, I have sensed a meeting of the minds with Richard Joyce (2001) and Hans-Georg Moeller (2009). Moeller, like Garner too, has expertly picked up on the so-called "applied" possibilities of amorality. But it is Joyce with whom my own theoretical thinking most exactly jibes, methinks; for although I am an abolitionist and he a fictionalist about morality, we seem to agree that the deciding issues between these positions are empirical and hence beyond our professional ken to resolve. There is also great affinity to the pioneering work of Ian Hinckfuss (1987) and of course J. L. Mackie (1977), among others. Some of these people I have known by professional acquaintance, others only from reading them; but to all I feel I am in intellectual debt or synch.

I have in addition enjoyed extensive and/or intensive intellectual exchanges with many others. Tom Clark, an articulate defender of naturalism, was an early correspondent; it was a pleasure to dialogue with him, despite the inability of either of us to convince the other. Greg Simay was another to respond immediately upon my first coming out as an amoralist, providing both supportive and challenging commentary as well as practical advice. Howard Benditsky, Jack Davis, Jerome Shaffer, and John Troyer read the entire manuscript of *Bad Faith* and responded with comments and encouragement. An inquiry by Bill Lycan regarding my much earlier work on desire came at just the right moment to inspire my cultivating a desirist amorality (which he might or might not approve). Harvey Green, longtime friend and colleague, engaged me in discussion about my latest philosophical hobbyhorse, as others before it, with his usual mix of endorsement and skepticism. Ian Smith happened on the scene during my initial amoralist ravings and has ever since been the droll utilitarian moralist to my dour Kantian amoralist. I have come to treasure Ian's earnestness and conciseness, and also want to credit him with recognizing the rhetorical power of comparing moralist defenses to theological ones. Robert Bass, who reviewed the penultimate draft of the present work, has brought to bear on my ramblings his unparalleled critical acumen. Allan Saltzman continues to encourage my evolution with his friendship and his intuitive anticipation of my deepest cogitations. Melanie Stengel has made herself available to many an emergency call to bat about a new idea and offer spot-on suggestions. The late, great David Morris understood the essential thesis way before I did, but did not live to see me accept it. Matthew Liao understood at once and offered penetrating but sympathetic challenges. Rob Irvine came across my work and has proved a most insightful interpreter and booster. Vera Huffman reached out as well and, with her persistence and acuteness, has become a valued interlocutor. Rhys Southan similarly happened upon my writing and seized the opportunity for a mutually satisfying and respectful dialogue based on an agreement to disagree about one particular "applied" issue. Maxim Fetissenko came to my attention with the publication of his excellent study of the rhetoric of morality, and I have since been benefiting from and enjoying his precision in conversation and correspondence. Huibing He abides with my every thought due to her insistence that I devote my life to the most fundamental things.

There have also been countless thoughtful bloggers and other commentators on my initial manifestoes on amorality, most of whom I simply did not have the time to reply to or in many cases even read or, I surmise, discover. Such are the fruits of the Internet Age.

Meanwhile, another whole realm of thought, and a story in its own right, has been my development as an animal ethicist. As suggested above, this played a crucial role in the motivating crisis that resulted first in my memoir and now this monograph. Perhaps I shall write a book on that subject, in whose Acknowledgments I could give suitable recognition to those who have guided me on this path. Here I will only mention that I owe a great debt to Lee Hall, Gary Francione, Justin Goodman, Eitan Fischer, Marc Bekoff, Colin Allen, Sue Leary, Wayne Pacelle, Larry Carbone, David Katz, Parker Shipton, Hal Herzog, Carol Pollard, David Smith, Susan Kopp, Stephen Latham, Thomas Murray, and, again, to Melanie Stengel, Wendell Wallach, Ian Smith, Robert Bass, and Maxim Fetissenko. And to many others who have spoken to and participated in the Animal Ethics Group at the Interdisciplinary Center for Bioethics at Yale University or have written in this field or have communicated with me. As well, to the editors

xvi *Acknowledgments*

of various journals, periodicals, blogs, and newspapers where I have held forth, including Gregory Kaebnick and Susan Gilbert (*Bioethics Forum*), Andrew Linzey (*Journal of Animal Ethics*), Joseph Lynch (*Between the Species*), Charles Kochakian (*New Haven Register*), and Peter Catapano and James Ryerson (*The New York Times*).

But how could any of my thinking have developed, about animals or amorality or anything else, if not for the invaluable forum provided me by Rick Lewis, Anja Steinbauer, and Grant Bartley, editors of *Philosophy Now*? For over a decade my columns have been a regular feature of this groundbreaking magazine, which seeks to put the most abstruse of subjects into plain language for nonprofessional and professional philosophers alike. And here it was that I first announced my amoral epiphany (or anti-epiphany, as I called it elsewhere), to the astonishment and, to some, consternation of my constant readers.

Once again I have relied on the extraordinary attentiveness of Evelina Woodruff, Library Technical Assistant at the University of New Haven's Marvin K. Peterson Library, in obtaining journal articles. And of course, much appreciation to my editors and readers at Routledge for their faith in this project and utter professionalism in bringing it to press.

Thank you to all.

Introduction

For some people, morality is part of the landscape. It needs no proof of existence, no more than does the furniture of the world we normally inhabit, including the literal furniture on which you now sit. No more than does God for the religious person who, like Tevye in *Fiddler on the Roof*, talks to Him on a regular basis. Some things we simply know, whether through the evidence of our senses or from the naturalness of thinking it so. When somebody cuts you off on the highway, you may react spontaneously: "Bastard!" This person has done something *wrong*. There are no two ways about it. If you are riled enough, you might wish this person dead; you might fantasize that his reckless actions will result in his car being wrapped around a tree just up ahead, and good riddance! Somebody who does something wrong deserves to be punished. It's all part of the scheme of things, as surely as an object dropped from a window will fall to the ground at 32 feet per second per second.

I don't believe this anymore. What don't I believe? I don't believe that morality exists in the way the chair you are sitting in does, or the way the gravity that cradles you in that chair exists. Morality does exist as a human institution, the way theistic religion exists. But, like God, it does not exist apart from our beliefs and feelings about it; it is not real in its own right. I could say therefore, to coin a term, that I no longer believe in *moreality*. Moreality is a universe in which moral right and wrong are as real as chairs and gravity. Even if everybody were like me and did not believe in morality, in *moreality* it would exist, just as surely as the earth is spherical even if everybody believed it was disc-shaped. But I now think moreality is a mythical realm because morality is a figment (unlike the sphericity of the earth). Morality is like the rule that Santa Claus will bring you toys if you are nice but not naughty. Many children believe this rule, and think that they live in a universe where Santa acts accordingly; but the universe is not like that because there is no such rule in reality. Parents sometimes play the role of Santa, and society, law courts, our own consciences sometimes play the role of morality. But however functional these role players may be, they are playing pretend if they purport to represent something other than themselves.

2   Ethics without Morals

This is a startling claim, at least for people who think they live in moreality. I was one of those people, which is why I am motivated to write this book. I write it not only to convince others of the truth of what I say but also to convince myself. For while I am now as sure as sure can be that morality does not exist (in the manner I have characterized), I was previously just as sure that it did. So I must be on my guard lest I have only been trading convictions rather than truth for falsity. I am like the person waking from a dream who is not yet quite sure where the dream leaves off and the world begins. I am still rubbing my eyes, both to remove the fog of sleep and to make sure that what I am seeing now is real, because it seems stranger than the dream.

I also believe that it is important to believe that morality does not exist. Why? For two main reasons: because truth matters, or at least can be very interesting, and because believing this particular truth, that morality does not exist, will makes things go better . . . or so I claim. Since I am a philosopher, I will strive to back up my claims with arguments, and to do so in the context of dialogue. Ideally you and I would be going back and forth with comments and responses, but because we are not in that position, I will instead try to anticipate your questions and counterarguments and answer all of them.

I must point out at once that everything in this book will be highly subjective. To my mind this is a harmless enough statement since I believe that everything in our experience is subjective. But you may not believe it (yet). So that is yet another claim I will need to defend . . . and in the first place, explain. Let me begin: One thing I mean by "subjective" is that every term, such as "morality," or for that matter "subjective," has a meaning for me that could be different from the meaning it has for you. So I will need to clarify what I am talking about at every step. Furthermore, this book is subjective because of its pervasive relativity. Thus, for example, when I wrote that "truth matters," what I really meant was that truth matters *to me* and, I suspect, *to you* and *to most people*.

These two senses of subjectivity correspond to two methods of doing philosophy. The first is the conceptual method or the analyzing of the meanings of words. The second is the empirical method or the adducing of facts about the world. You might suppose that the second belongs to science rather than philosophy, but I see a distinction between the establishing of facts and the adducing of facts. I will allow science (in addition to everyday experience) pride of place in the former, but once that task has been accomplished, philosophy takes over. That is to say: Once something has been accepted as fact, then we can adduce that fact in support of further claims, or the establishing of further facts, if you will.

Ultimately the distinction between the two methods may not stand. After all, in analyzing the meaning of a word, are we not also implicitly engaging in an empirical investigation? If I analyzed "cat" as a four-legged mammal that barks, wouldn't a scientific study of word usage count against it? I accept that conclusion (both the particular one and the general one). So all I really mean by conceptual investigation is a kind of armchair empiricism about language use. This in turn helps to unify the meaning of "philosophy" itself as the adducing of already known facts in support of claims about . . . whatever.[1] Those facts may have become known through scientific investigation, or they may simply be part of the store of facts we feel confident about without need of scientific backing. It may be somewhat unclear in a given case which sort of fact is being adduced; so, do we know that "cat" means "four-legged mammal that meows" via a scientific lexicography or linguistics, or do we know it just from everyday experience? Most formal philosophy is indifferent about that. For one thing, both types of knowledge could be "common knowledge," since some truths of science, such as that the earth is round, can be just as well known as the truths we "pick up" from daily existence, such as that oranges are round.[2] In the body of this book I will tend to rely on what I take to be common knowledge (for you and me), but I will supplement that with reference to more technical knowledge (or argument) in the notes.

With respect to the matter at hand, I will argue for a particular meaning of the word "morality," and then I will defend the further claims that morality (in that sense) does not exist and that it would be good for us to believe that. An example of *how something with a meaning may yet not exist and it be good for us to know that* is the notion of a witch as a sorceress with evil magic powers.[3] There are no such beings, and it is good for society to believe that so that we won't go around burning innocent women. I believe that what most people think of as morality is like that kind of witch. Now let me try to convince you of that.

Note on the title (*Ethics without Morals*): Despite being a defense of amorality, this inquiry remains an ethical one, for it addresses the questions, "What is morality?" and "How shall one live?" That the answers are, respectively, *a myth* and *without that myth*,[4] does not change the fact. More particularly, the title was inspired by the title of a recent collection of essays edited by Louise M. Antony—*Philosophers without Gods* (Oxford University Press, 2007)—since the theme of that book is really that there are *moralists* without God,[5] whereas I want to take the argument one step further to conclude that there can be ethicists who are neither theists nor moralists.

Note on style: I prefer dialogue to scholarship and academese; I want to have a conversation with you in common and contemporary terms, and without name-dropping or disciplinary jargon.[6] Also, I admit, I enjoy being a writer more than being a scholar; for me this means pulling all ideas and all formulations of them out of my own skull rather than by direct reference to published sources.[7] On the other hand, I wish to give credit where it is due and, even more fundamentally, not simply reinvent the wheel or assert things that have already been roundly refuted. So I have decided to split the difference by confining all scholarly references to notes. This also makes for a smoother read of the main text.

1 What Is Morality?

> God's in his Heaven–
> All's right with the world![1]

As surely as up and down, dark and light, our world contains right and wrong ... *saith the moralist*. We can simply see that a balloon is rising or that dusk is descending or that Fagin's corruption of a child is wrong. God's in his heaven, and, while not all is right with the world, ever since our fall from grace we have judged almost everything on Earth to be *either* right or wrong, good or evil, pious or impious[2] ... just as, before acquiring that fatal knowledge, we had named[3] "every beast of the field, and every fowl of the air."[4] Our common conception of morality, therefore, is of something real and pervasive, if perhaps also a little hot for us humans to handle.

Exactly how commonly held this conception is,[5] is an empirical question, which I will leave to the social scientists to answer definitively.[6] Morality may be peculiar to Western civilization,[7] or it may only be the preoccupation of theologians and academic philosophers of a certain stripe. What I can assert with confidence is that I myself believed in a morality of this sort; and when I did, it seemed clear to me that my belief was widely, indeed universally, shared. Although I am now skeptical on both counts—that is, I now believe that the belief in morality is neither universally accepted nor even true—I still sense that it is widely enough held, and with sufficiently baneful influence on the world, that going to some effort to dispel it would be a worthwhile undertaking. But it is clear that I cannot simply ask, "What do we mean by 'morality'?" since it would always be meet for someone to inquire in turn, "Who are 'we'?" As I continue to characterize the concept in this chapter, you will have to judge for yourself whether or to what degree this book is addressed to you and to the world.[8]

So what is this thing called morality? I have always taken it to be a set of absolute and universal imperatives and prohibitions, the Biblical Ten Commandments being paradigmatic in the West. Morality has a lawlike structure, but in the way of human rather than scientific laws. In other words, the moral law does not act on us directly, the way the law of gravity determines the rate of our descent in a free fall.[9] Instead it acts via the intermediary of our will, so that "Thou shalt not bear false witness against thy neighbor" does not guarantee that you won't lie but only solicits your voluntary compliance. This is just how a speed limit works, or a criminal law against murder. Neither can stop you from committing the infraction without the concurrence of your will to refrain. The difference between the human law and the moral law, however, is that the latter is infallible and universal. Human laws can and do vary from country to country and era to era because they are the products of human beings situated in a culture and possessed of vying interests. By contrast, moral law is, or is as it were, the product of divine fiat; it emanates from an unchanging and univocal font—of wisdom and beneficence, one would like to think, but at least of authority and power.

When I look into my own moral heart I discern fear more than respect or love for this One God of Right and Wrong. I cower before my conscience. Sometimes conscience speaks to me with what seems simple reasonableness. But at other times it just pronounces, so I am not asked to agree but only to obey. Curiously, however, there are yet other occasions when I am filled with a moral emotion emanating only from myself, and that emotion could be compassion or anger. I then myself become the god, who wants assistance to be tendered to the unfortunate or punishment meted out to the evildoer. Even so, with only this internal bidding, the feeling or judgment retains an absolute and universal character; I would expect every right-thinking soul to share my emotion or opinion, and I would feel a further, condemnatory emotion toward someone who failed to.

The above account makes frequent reference to God or a god. Could we say, then, that morality is equivalent to religiosity or piety? At this point philosophy diverges from theology. The former sees "piety" as simply a way of being moral. In its most well-known formulation,[10] the philosophical view takes piety to be allegiance not to God so much as to God's unerring understanding of what is good or right on independent grounds. That is to say: It is not just God's declaring something to be (morally) right that makes it so, but right's *being* right that makes God declare it so. In the same way, the fact that 2+2=4 made your arithmetic teacher's assertion of it correct, rather than *vice versa*; so if your teacher had told you that 2+2=5, your teacher would have been mistaken.[11]

Just so, according to the philosophic notion of piety, if a voice inside your head told you to murder your innocent son, you would have clear grounds to doubt that that voice came from God, because God would never tell you to do something wrong, and it would be wrong to murder your innocent son. Moreover, since religion as it is commonly presented in the Abrahamic traditions, condones, indeed glories in Abraham's willingness to "sacrifice" Isaac,[12] the philosophic piety of which I speak eventually decayed into a pure secularity of morality. Philosophical ethics became the pursuit of grounds independent of either God's fiat or God's instruction for telling the difference between what we should do and what we should not do. Thus, ironically, secular ethics seeks to replicate the religious origin of sin (of wresting the knowledge of good and evil from God's providence).[13]

It is interesting to consider how morality relates, then, to decision making as such. After all, terms like "should" and "ought" have applications outside of morality. Wherever there are norms or standards, there is *should* (and also *right* and *wrong*). You *should* use an apostrophe in the contraction of "it" and "is"; it is the grammatically right thing to do. You *should* take an umbrella if it looks like heavy weather outside; that would be the prudentially right thing to do. You *should* use a hammer if you want to drive in a nail; that would be the pragmatically right thing to do. You *should* drive on the left side of the road in England; that would be the legally (as well as prudentially and morally) right thing to do.

So what distinguishes the *moral* should? Observe that one kind of *should* can trump another; for example, on a given occasion the grammatical rule to use "isn't" for "is not" could be *over*-ruled by a rhetorical justification to use "ain't." My conception of morality is as the highest *telos*,[14] by which I mean that the morally right thing to do is supposed to be what we should do "all short" (*tout court*) or *simpliciter* or "in the last analysis" or "all things considered." Thus, the moral *should* trumps all others, and at all times and everywhere.[15]

Considered in this way, morality would seem to be equivalent to practical rationality, for once we have figured out what we ought to do according to morality, we could plausibly be supposed to have gauged, simultaneously and in the nature of the case, what reason would dictate as well. Could there be a conflict between reason and morals? Could, for example, lying on some particular occasion be morally wrong and yet the rational thing to do? If you think not, then it naturally seems to follow that one way to determine what is the right, or at least a permissible[16] thing to do, would be to figure out what it is rational to do. This way of thinking about morality has appealed to many philosophers, who love reason to begin with.[17]

But here we have come upon one of those "vexed questions" that keep philosophers philosophizing perennially. For as much as we may be drawn to the idea of moral living as the epitome of rational living, we also have intuitions militating against their identity. For one thing, even if the moral thing to do were always rational, it would not follow automatically that the rational thing to do was always moral. There are three reasons for this. One is pure logic: From *if p then q*, it does not follow that *if q then p*. For example, it is plausible to maintain that everything that has a color also has a shape, or "*if* x has a color, *then* x has a shape." But the converse does not follow, because you could have a square piece of untinted glass. Just so, even if everything that was moral turned out to be rational, there might be some things that it was rational to do but not moral to do.[18]

The second reason to doubt the equivalence of morality and rationality is (as alluded to earlier) that "moral" is ambiguous between "morally right" and "morally permissible."[19] If something were moral in the latter sense, then it would not be wrong to do it. But if something were moral in the sense of being the right thing to do, then it would be *obligatory*—in other words, wrong *not* to do it. And third, the analogous is true of rationality: "Rational" can mean either rationally permissible or rationally obligatory, the latter being the right thing to do rationally speaking. For example, reason may *dictate* that you not lean your hand on the hot burner, but only *allow* that you choose vanilla over chocolate ice cream, given that you like them both equally (and "all other things equal"); the latter would be rational simply in virtue of not being irrational.

So when we ask whether morality and rationality always go hand in hand, we could be asking any of several different things, namely: (1) Is every morally obligatory act rationally obligatory? (2) Is every morally obligatory act rationally permissible? (3) Is every morally permissible act rationally permissible? (4) Is every morally permissible act rationally obligatory? (5) Is every rationally obligatory act morally obligatory? (6) Is every rationally obligatory act morally permissible? (7) Is every rationally permissible act morally permissible? (8) Is every rationally permissible act morally obligatory? (If the reader's eyes have just begun to glaze over, you may skip the six following paragraphs and resume reading at "*Ergo*.")

The answer to (8) seems clearly to be "No": The ice cream example settles that. It is a matter of rational indifference which flavor you choose, and, far from being morally obligatory (or "moral" or "right" *tout court*), hardly a moral issue at all. (5) is also easily decided: It could be rationally compelling (as always: "all other things equal") for you to go out to eat because you were hungry and there was nothing in the cupboard, and furthermore it might be perfectly permissible (morally or "*tout court*") for you to do so, there being no conflicting urgent moral demand placed upon you, such as performing CPR on a stricken roommate; but in the run of cases it would certainly not be your moral *obligation* to go out to eat just because you were hungry and hadn't gone food shopping lately. Therefore even though you have, as it were, a *rational* obligation to go out to eat, you are not, in the last analysis, obligated to do so, for morality, which trumps all else, does not require that you do so. Therefore the answer to (5) is also "No."

But how about (6): Would a rationally obligatory act always be at least morally permissible? I think "No" again, although this is a more interesting question. Suppose you have learned that a bundle of cash is stashed on a yacht anchored in the harbor and decide to steal it. The next day under cover of darkness you swim to the boat when you think no one is on board, climb in, grab the bundle, scuttle the boat to cover the crime, and then leap overboard. As you are about to swim back to shore with your precious booty, you hear someone shout: "You took that! I saw you!" You look back and notice a small boy on the deck. Meanwhile the boat is taking on water, and the boy suddenly notices. "I can't swim!" he cries. Soon the water is swirling around you both. The boy is floundering helplessly. You realize that he will drown unless you rescue him. But you cannot grab hold of him and hold onto the bundle of money at the same time. The choice is yours: Save the life of the one person who can incriminate you and lose your ill-gotten gains in the bargain, or solve both problems simply by going about your business.

Clearly it would be morally impermissible to let the boy drown. But it also seems plausible to maintain that it would be irrational for you to save him.[20] If in the end you do "make the right choice," it will have been the *morally* right choice, but not the one that prudence would have dictated.[21] And, curiously, reason does seem to ally itself more with prudence than with morality. So in rescuing the child you would be listening to your conscience rather than reason. Oh yes, there could be reasons to save the child, such as to avoid an even worse "rap" of manslaughter than of robbery if you were ever caught; and the boy might even "cover" for you out of gratitude (or fear). Furthermore, you might have to live with a "guilty conscience" if you didn't rescue him. But these things—some bad feelings, risk of punishment—might be viewed by you as the cost of doing business, your business being burglary, which, on balance, has a bigger payoff for you than an honest job and a clear conscience. Therefore, again, the answer to (6) is "No" because it is possible to be rational and immoral at the same time.

(7) has now also been decided, since if something is obligatory, then it is surely permissible; yet, as we have just seen, a rationally obligatory act will not necessarily be morally permissible; therefore, all the more, a merely rationally permissible act need not be morally permissible either. So the answer to (7) is "No": and since "No" is the answer to (5), (6), and (8) as well, rationality does not imply morality, no matter which sense of "moral" or "rational" one has in mind.

This leaves (1)—(4): Does morality imply rationality? I think we can swiftly rule on (4) and assert that the answer is "No" again: Something could be morally permissible without being rationally obligatory. I may decide to buy a pair of checkered pants on whim, which we may suppose is barely rationally supportable, but, all other things equal, I will have done nothing morally prohibited. Is morality so tolerant as to allow my doing something that is not rational at all? Suppose my purchasing those checkered pants will scotch my prospects with the lady I have my eye on, whose attentions mean far more to me than those particular pants: Would morality as well as rationality put its foot down? I think not. Morality could (i.e., *couldn't*) care less about my romantic outlook. Therefore the answer to (3) is also "No."

This brings us finally to the question of the rationality of moral obligation. If there is something that you morally must do, i.e., must do *tout court*, will you of necessity be doing something rational? No! In fact we already saw this with the drowning boy example. For in establishing that something that is rationally obligatory (not rescuing the boy) can nevertheless be morally impermissible, we have at the same time shown that something can be morally obligatory (rescuing the boy) even though it would be rationally impermissible. Hence the answer to (2) is "No." And if it would be rationally impermissible it would certainly not be rationally obligatory, so the answer to (1) is also "No."

Ergo: Morality does not imply rationality, no matter which sense of "moral" one has in mind. And we have previously established that rationality does not imply morality, no matter which sense of "moral" one has in mind. Therefore morality and rationality are not as closely linked as might have been supposed. Perhaps the reason this comes as a surprise is that, even though they are certainly distinct conceptually, they are both highly esteemed.[22] It is rather the way we should be perplexed to find Mahatma Gandhi and Mother Teresa getting into a scuffle. But this could also *explain* their *pairing*, since we tend to lavish honorifics, to the point of gratuitousness, on things (and people) we esteem (as we similarly heap aspersions on those we scorn). The bottom line is that, while both morality and rationality are values, they are different values, and so it will always be possible for them to diverge or even conflict. In this respect they are like mercy and justice or duty and happiness. In a perfect world there might be no such conflicts, but this is not that world.

But what have I really established about morality? Maybe nothing! First let me remind you that in this chapter I am only talking about the concept of morality. So anything I assert or conclude about morality herein is like asserting that Bigfoot lives in the Pacific Northwest: This could be "true" whether or not there really is a Bigfoot. But secondly, even with regard to the concept, there may not be such a thing as *the* concept. Maybe some people conceive of Bigfoot as *essentially* nonhuman, such that if a big hairy fellow were found in the Northwest woods who was undeniably human, that would not be Bigfoot; whereas just as many people might conceive Bigfoot as *essentially* a particular human who "went native" after crashing his airplane, so that if some rogue gorilla were found, that would not be Bigfoot. So what I am doing first and foremost in this chapter is to characterize morality as it seems intuitively to be to me, the author; and when I say "to be to me," I mean both as I myself tend to conceive morality *and* as I take *most other people* to.

Furthermore, this characterization is "warts and all." So there could be a multiplicity within this conception, even conflict. There are several possible sources of that: My personal conception could be manifold, the conceptions I take others to have could be similarly manifold, and/or all of our conceptions could differ one from another. I have already mentioned how I see morality as emanating sometimes from an external authority and at other times from my own authority. I will also discuss below how considerations of consequences can vie with considerations of duty.

What all of this suggests is that a disagreement about the concept or nature of morality does not necessarily imply that one conception is correct and another incorrect. Perhaps another way to put the same point is that I am *not* attempting to offer a definitive statement, or *theory*, of what morality is. In fact, since my ultimate aim in this book is to get rid of morality, it would not be terribly upsetting to me to discover that the very concept of morality is hopelessly elusive or even confused.[23] That right there could be the grounds for denying its utility and hence for discarding it. The situation might therefore be analogous to trying to liberate some cult of its preoccupation with preparing for the incarnation of the Four-Sided Triangle, or, alternatively, to the medical diagnosis of "shock" during World War II, which was so diverse that it became unintelligible and even dangerous due to the misunderstandings that could thereby result.[24]

I do think there is something like that going on with morality. For instance, it could be argued that there is an incoherence at the very heart of morality because, on the one hand, we tend to think of the slogan "Might makes right" as an ironical expression of the antithesis of morality, yet on the other hand, when challenged to explicate the meaning of the moral *should*, many people can come up with nothing better than our duty to yield to an Absolute Power.

But I won't make my case against morality by arguing for its incoherence. I am content to accept that morality does have a widely accepted meaning that is intelligible—or that is as intelligible as any concept is in the world of everyday experience.[25] In this chapter, then, I am content to sketch the conception of morality that seems best to capture the one that I myself hold and believe many if not most people hold; but the sketch has rough edges, smudges, and gaps . . . just as the conception does.[26] This should no more preclude our finally definitively rejecting morality than, say, our not being able to give a full accounting of Sherlock Holmes' childhood or decide whether his personality is clinically introverted, prevents our confidently denying his historical existence.

So far my sketch looks like this: Morality is the set of imperatives (and/or truths about what we should do) that apply to all human beings of all climes and times, that trump all others, and that manifest in our feelings, either as commands to be obeyed, as if from an external Power or Authority, or simply as spontaneous promptings of the "heart" or "guts." We have also seen that morality is distinct from rationality on one hand and theological piety on the other; the dictates of all three can and do diverge one from the other. Does this suffice for the purpose of debunking its existence? Note in particular that nothing definitive has been said about the precise content of morality, but only its general form has been characterized. In other words, morality tells us what to do and not to do; but what, exactly, are we to do or not to do? For all that has been observed so far, it could be moral to lie, cheat, pillage, rape, and murder.[27]

Technically speaking we are now entering the realm of normative ethics, whereas previously we were occupied with meta-ethics. The distinction is somewhat analogous to a biological taxonomy, as between genus and species. As there are mammals and then types of mammals, so there is morality and then there are various types of morality.[28] Meta-ethics is the branch of ethics that deals with the broader category of morality as such, and normative ethics with the narrower category of a particular type of morality. One difference between biology and ethics, however, is that the various types of morality are competitive rather than complementary. It is perfectly fine that there are lions and tigers and bears, but it is usually deemed problematic that there are Aristotelians, Benthamites, and Kantians (oh my!).

Why is this a problem? One could attempt to answer that question in two very different ways. One way would be internal to the discipline of ethics and give an ethical accounting of why morality must be of a single type. For instance, to have a cafeteria of moral theories is to invite the selection of whichever one best suits one's selfish motives. But it is a desideratum or requirement of morality that it not lend itself readily to our selfish tendencies. Therefore there is a moral reason for morality to be monotypic. Alternatively or in addition, one could point to the potential for conflict whenever there are multiple mandates; for example, if it were wrong to mislead and wrong to hurt someone's feelings, what would be your obligation when being honest would hurt someone's feelings? So another desideratum of morality is to preclude moral dilemmas, which suggests that there must be a fundamental theory that would break all "ties" among less fundamental principles. Meanwhile, a more straightforward way to support the notion of a single moral type would be to defend one's favored moral theory as capable of explaining all of our particular moral intuitions. The latter in fact is precisely the normal business of normative ethics.

But one could also argue, externally to the discipline of ethics, that moralists tend to favor a single moral theory as another symptom of whatever it is that drives some of us human beings to favor one God over many gods. This would be a psychologizing or psychoanalyzing of ethics. But there could also be an anthropology or a sociology of why, say, Western culture has had this kind of mono-mindset.[29] There might even simply be a *history* to be told; for example, perhaps the supposedly secular ethicists have in fact internalized the monotheism of their religious heritage and, for this reason alone, regardless of their meta-ethical rationales and physics-like theorizing, have seen their task to be the articulation and defense of The One True Morality. Thus, monotheism begat monotheorism.

I myself am first and foremost a philosopher, and to me that means, among other things, questioning fundamental assumptions, even those of philosophy or ethics. So I present the theories below in a catholic spirit: They might *all* be constitutive of "our" conception of morality, however messy and even corrupting that fact might be. What I am resisting is the (common philosophical) tendency to legislate or "reform" morality to fit onto the Procrustean bed of a single ideal.[30] To repeat: It is not that I believe "anything goes" as to what would count as moral. I simply happen to believe that the prevailing conception of morality is smudgy and multifaceted. So there can be occasions when someone is mistaken—or "wrong" in the sense of harboring a false belief—about whether something is, say, morally permissible (torturing babies),[31] or even a moral issue to begin with (shining your shoes); but there could also be occasions when this is indeterminate (Is it morally permissible to kill an innocent person who will otherwise inadvertently cause a catastrophe? Is it even a moral issue whether to rush into a burning building in a desperate attempt to rescue an occupant?[32]).

The essential core of morality, as I understand it, remains its universal, unchanging,[33] and absolute authority in matters of human behavior. If a candidate for morality did not have this feature, then it would be running for the wrong office. Nevertheless, there could be, and are many candidates that satisfy this condition, yet each with its own additional set of features that have intuitive appeal. For example, the so-called principle of utility[34] is often put forward as inherent to morality: The right thing to do is that which will maximize welfare or happiness.[35] Alternatively, the so-called categorical imperative[36] exhorts us never to treat any person merely as a means. And of course the Golden Rule advises that we do unto others as we would have them do unto us. It is possible "in the abstract" that all of these claims to moral truth amount to the same thing. But the tendency among moral philosophers has been to drive wedges between them and seek to vindicate one over the others. This effort involves spelling out the full meaning of each to suit the distinctiveness and superiority of the favored one. I have covered that ground elsewhere,[37] and it is not germane to my main thesis in the present book; so I won't go over it again.

What I will do instead is draw upon various such claims to flesh out morality as I conceive it now. For the most part I go with the categorical imperative or Kantianism (after its great expositor, Immanuel Kant). It has long seemed to me to capture what morality is all about, which is to say, what is really moving me when I react to something with a moral emotion or attitude or judgment. For example, what is it exactly about that fellow cutting me off on the highway that churns my gut with moral indignation? Is it that he is putting me at risk? Is it that he is acting recklessly? Is it that he is acting selfishly or foolishly? Well, all of those things are part of it, of course. But one could imagine reacting to those various aspects of the case with different emotions and judgments from the moral one.

In fact all of the descriptors just listed are nonmoral ones: risky, reckless, foolish, even selfish. A person or an action could be any or all of them without being immoral or eliciting moral condemnation. If I reached too far for the last apple on the tree when my basket was already overfull, I could be acting riskily, recklessly, foolishly, and selfishly, without doing anything morally wrong; and an observer might be amused rather than angered as I toppled from the ladder, or solicitous of my welfare if she thought I were injured, or simply disinterested. Even if, as in the highway case, the risk were being imposed on another, the situation could be morally kosher; for example, tossing your child out of a burning building could put him at grave risk, yet be permissible, even obligatory.

What turns all of these morally neutral descriptors into moral factors in the highway incident, it seems to me, is their use to characterize a violation of the categorical imperative. That driver was riskily, recklessly, foolishly, and selfishly *treating me as a mere means* to his end of reaching his destination quickly. We could also say: He was failing to respect me as a person. My welfare, my goals, my destination were as nothing to him. He effectively assigned them zero value in his scheme of things.[38] It was, speaking autobiographically, an amazing revelation to me when I realized—thanks to Immanuel Kant—that there was this simplifying, unifying way to understand the vast diversity of phenomena that elicit my moral disapproval. It was quite analogous to Newton's fixing on gravity as the common cause of the planets staying in their courses, the tides washing up at his feet, and the apple hitting him on the noggin. I came to appreciate that everything from lying to stealing to raping to killing was wrong (if and when it was wrong), not because it was lying or stealing or raping or killing, and not because it hurt someone or snubbed someone or deceived someone, etc., but solely and precisely because it involved treating somebody merely as a means.[39]

And yet I cannot deny that there are occasions when a different principle appeals to my intuition and may even trump the categorical imperative. The principle of utility or utilitarianism (whose great expositor was John Stuart Mill) is the main contender here: Maximize the good. Consider the decision by Chinese authorities to limit every family to one child as a way to curb overpopulation in their severely impoverished country.[40] This tramples on one of the most basic human rights: to be fruitful and multiply. Yet my "intuitive sense" is that it was right to adopt and implement this policy because it seems likely to bring about a much better state of affairs than not doing so. Certainly it was rational and prudent. Was it moral? Well, if moral means to avoid treating people as mere means, then apparently not; for the desires and interests of many individual Chinese citizens were being ignored in order to better the lot of future generations. But since the decision seems right to me nevertheless, as the thing to do, indeed, imperative to do, all things considered, then the moral criterion by which I am judging it must be a utilitarian one.

It is important to note that the utilitarian principle is also categorical. Here we encounter a potential source of terminological confusion. I have indicated that I tend to favor the normative theory of Immanuel Kant, which often goes by the name of the "categorical imperative." But there is another meaning of categorical imperative, also attributable to Kant,[41] which applies to moral injunctions as such; in other words, the term has a meta-ethical sense as well as a normative one. *All* moral commands (or truths) are categorical in the sense of being non-hypothetical; another term for this is "absolute," as opposed to relative, and yet another, "objective," as opposed to subjective or dependent on belief or desire. Thus, even though the principle of utility is a distinct criterion of moral rightness from the normative categorical imperative, *both* criteria are categorical imperatives in the sense of commanding unconditionally and independently of whether anyone happens to be happy about it.[42]

14 *Ethics without Morals*

As the meta-ethical notion of categoricalness is crucial to my case against morality, it bears further elaboration. Consider the following arguments for how we ought to behave according to three distinct normative standards: grammar, prudence, and morality.

> Grammatically speaking, the right thing to do is to use "isn't" instead of "ain't" for the contraction of "is not."
> Therefore (you should) never use "ain't" for the contraction of "is not."

> Prudentially speaking, the right thing to do is to avoid unnecessary risk.
> Therefore (you should) never assume unnecessary risk.

> Morally speaking, it is wrong to deceive someone for purely personal benefit.
> Therefore (you should) never deceive someone for purely personal benefit.

What is distinctive about the third argument is that the "speaking" qualification in the premise could be dropped without affecting the meaning. I only inserted it to expose the moral nature of the argument, thereby to distinguish it from the two other arguments; but the first premise of the third argument is intended to apply *sans phrase*. In the other arguments, however, the qualification is essential. Why? *Because it reveals the invalidity of those inferences*. After all, just because something is a rule of grammar does not imply that it is mandatory *in all cases*; as noted previously, there could be on some occasion, for example, a good rhetorical reason to forsake grammar. And just because something may be imprudent does not mean that one ought never to undertake it; indeed, it is easy enough to imagine being *morally* obligated to do something that was *supremely* imprudent.[43] But if something is morally wrong, then one may conclude straightaway that one ought not to do it, "period."[44]

A different way to make the same point would be to convert all three of the above arguments into explicitly valid inferences by inserting an additional premise (which exposes what had been merely assumed),[45] thus:

> Grammatically speaking, the right thing to do is to use "isn't" instead of "ain't" for the contraction of "is not."
> *One should always do the grammatical thing.*
> Therefore (you should) never use "ain't" for the contraction of "is not."
>
> Prudentially speaking, the right thing to do is to avoid unnecessary risk.
> *One should always do the prudent thing.*
> Therefore (you should) never assume unnecessary risk.

Morally speaking, it is wrong to deceive someone for purely personal benefit.
One should always do the moral thing.
Therefore (you should) never deceive someone for purely personal benefit.

The categoricalness of morality is the assertion or assumption of the truth of this added premise in the third argument. Now, a strict grammarian might indeed feel just as strongly about the added premise in the first argument; but I doubt that this would meet with common acceptance, even among writers. And while an extremely cautious personality might warm to the added premise in the *second* argument, most of us would give it no more credence than we would the strict grammarian's principle. But the added premise of the third argument is not only unexceptionable to the moralist but a seeming analytic truth: the very meaning of "the morally right thing to do" is that one should do it.

The categoricalness of morality is not itself, however, a moral assertion. One is not answering the question, "Why do the morally right thing?" or "Why be moral?" by saying, "Because it is the morally right thing to do." That would only beg the question and get us nowhere. This is why we speak of *meta-ethics* as a realm distinct from morality itself. The categoricalness of morality comes to us as a brute fact of the universe, which we intuit. If morality turns out to be equivalent to Kantianism or to utilitarianism or to both (or to some other, etc.), then we know this because we intuit *their* categoricalness specifically. The relevant moral principle then tells us what is the right or wrong thing to do in particular types of situations; for example, when faced with the prospect of purely personal gain by means of deception, do not deceive, because to deceive for personal gain would violate the categorical principle never to treat anyone merely as a means.

My account of morality still leaves many questions unanswered. But recall again that I am not trying to resolve all moral (or meta-moral) issues in this chapter, not only because of space considerations, but chiefly because my final position is that morality does not exist. So while I am certainly trying to give morality its best shot here so as not to be setting up a straw person, I am not going to go out of my way to dot every "i". In the end, I would view that as an idle exercise, given my intent to understand reality and not merely limn an elaborate fairy tale.

The main point I have wished to establish in this chapter is that, whatever the precise "content" of morality, its "form" is categorical. Admittedly I have not so much established the truth of this claim as sketched its meaning. It remains an empirical question, beyond the competence of this inquiry to decide, how widely this conception of morality is held. My assumption is that it is the prevailing view, but in any case, it is what I mean when I talk about morality.[46]

2 Does Morality Exist?

Once upon a time we believed that 2+2=4, the earth is round, and lying is wrong. Today we still believe that 2+2=4 and the earth is round, but some of us deny that lying is wrong. It is not that we deniers believe that lying is right *or even permissible*. Rather, we—call us *amoralists*[1]—view this sort of right and wrong as *mythical*, so that nothing has these properties in reality.

A helpful analogy, at least for an atheist (as an amoralist typically is), is sin. Even though words like "sinful" and "evil" come as naturally to the tongue as a description of, say, child molesting, they do not describe any actual properties of anything. There are no literal sins in the world because there is no literal God to ground the religious superstructure that would include such categories as sin and evil. Or think of this nonreligious analogy: a tribe of people living on an isolated island who have no formal governmental institutions of any kind. In particular they have no legislature. Therefore in that society it would make no sense to say that someone had done something "illegal." But neither would anything be "legal." The entire set of legal categories would be inapplicable. In just this way I now view moral categories. Nothing is morally right or wrong or even merely permissible, because there is no morality.

Of course I am referring to morality as I have characterized it in the preceding chapter, namely, as a categorical imperative. There *is* such a thing as the *social institution* of morality. That is a phenomenon that can be studied by empirical science: sociology, anthropology, geography, economics, history. There are also beliefs and attitudes about morality, which can be studied by scientific psychology, and indeed by experimental philosophy.[2] But this is equally true of theistic religion, as even the atheist would concede. Nevertheless it can be meaningfully asserted that there is no God and there is no morality, and either or both assertions could be true.

My thesis in this chapter is that the second assertion is true: There is no such thing as morality.[3] But how would one go about defending that? Given the widespread belief in morality, the burden of proof would seem to be on the skeptic. I accept that, and offer as my methodology *inference to the best explanation*.[4] Its logic is this: It is rational to believe in x if and only if x is an element of our best explanation of the world as we know it. The argument for amorality is then simply that morality is not an element of our best explanation of the world as we know it.[5] More particularly: All of the familiar phenomena that we associate with morality—we could call them "empirical morality"—can be accounted for *without*, more plausibly than *by*, postulating the existence of morality in the sense that I have put forward as its common conception—call the latter "metaphysical morality" (or as I usually do in this book, simply "morality").

By the familiar phenomena of (empirical) morality I have in mind the beliefs and attitudes we hold about moral right and wrong and goodness and badness, our resultant feelings and motivations and behaviors, and the language we use to talk about it all. The general assumption of humanity (or the parts of it that recognize an institution of morality) is that all of these things owe their legitimacy and very existence to the reality of (metaphysical) morality.[6] I say that they have no legitimacy, precisely because there is no such reality. To revert to my analogy from the Introduction: The burning of (women labeled as) witches had no legitimacy precisely because there were no witches, i.e., beings with evil magical powers, despite the prevalent belief that there were. And we now recognize that all of the beliefs and attitudes about witches were due to ignorance and bigotry (plus a smattering of more sympathetic concerns, we could suppose as well). Just so, all of the phenomena of morality are readily explainable by mundane cause and effect.[7]

For example, we were brought up to believe that lying is something that God frowns upon and may punish you for doing or, God aside, that the universe itself, as it were, takes a dim view of lying, no matter who you are, when or where you lived, or what the circumstances. These beliefs are probably false. But even so we can explain why many of us believe that lying is wrong and feel a pang of conscience when we lie and sometimes tell the truth when we would rather not, etc. The straightforward explanation of these phenomena is simply that we have been brought up or "conditioned" to think, feel, and act in these ways. (And this explanation of our beliefs, etc., would apply even if our beliefs about morality were *true*.) A more extensive explanation is that the program of our upbringing or conditioning must serve some function in the story that biology has to tell about human evolution.

There are, then, three basic explanations typically offered for why we feel that some things are morally right, others wrong, and the rest simply permissible:

1. We have a faculty of conscience or intuition that enables us to perceive (or heed) the moral law(s) (or commands) that God has laid down (or issued).
2. We have a faculty of conscience or intuition that enables us to perceive (or heed) the moral law(s) (or commands) that inhere in (or

emanate from) the fabric of the universe itself, analogously to the laws of physics.
3. Belief in and adherence to moral laws or commands put us at some vital advantage in the competition for necessary but finite resources in our environment (physical or cultural).

The third explanation, which is Darwinian in nature, is, I claim, the best explanation of the three. So how does the argument for that claim go? It is actually a battery of arguments, but the basic structure of it is to discredit the two first explanations and then lay out the positive reasons we have for accepting the third.

I observe in passing that the three explanations are not necessarily incompatible. For example, the ultimate explanation might be that God created a universe in which inhere the moral laws and in which dwell creatures like ourselves, whose continued existence is contingent on our being attuned and responsive to those laws. So in arguing for only the last as the "best explanation," I am in effect wielding Occam's razor. This is because Explanation No. 3 would suffice to give us empirical morality in the absence of the two other explanations; therefore by an epistemic notion of economy we may or even should dispense with the latter.

One must use the Occamistic strategy with care, however. I am reminded of the following joke:[8]

> A religious skeptic asks a rabbi, "Rabbi, how can you think that your religious beliefs are correct? Don't you acknowledge that if you had been brought up in Rome . . . or Riyadh . . . you would have believed in Jesus or Allah?" To which the rabbi replies, "Yes, and therefore I thank God that I was brought up where I could know the truth—in Brooklyn!"

This is quite funny, but also penetrating and far-reaching if you think about it. For not only are our beliefs and feelings about religion contingent in this way, and even, as already noted, our beliefs and feelings about morality, but also all of our beliefs and feelings about anything whatever. Thus, not only do I believe that I am sitting at a computer and tapping on the keyboard as I compose this book, but I also believe that my belief that I am sitting at a computer, etc., was caused by (or may even metaphysically *be*) some neurons firing in my brain.[9] But this does not in the least preclude my believing that I am sitting at a computer. Yet shouldn't it? Following the logic of the rabbi joke: I also know that I could have the same belief (that I am sitting at a computer, etc.) due to dreaming it.

The philosophy of knowledge or epistemology has grappled with this sort of issue forever, and will continue to do so. For our purposes, suffice it to say that we do accept that sometimes we have knowledge and other times we are mistaken. In both cases, what we *believe* will have been caused by contingent factors, such as being taught something in school or mishearing what somebody said. The fact remains that sometimes what we believe is true and other times false.[10] The problem with the Occam's Razor objection to morality, then, is that it could rest on a flawed principle, namely, that anything in addition to the causal explanation of a phenomenon is dispensable. But this would rule out what makes any *belief true*. For the truth conditions of a belief are always external to the belief's cause. This applies to nonmoral beliefs as well as to moral beliefs, as the example of my believing I am sitting at my computer shows, since this belief is caused by neurons firing in my brain, regardless of whether I am actually at my computer, dreaming, or floating in a vat.[11]

But the above reasoning is itself flawed. It relies on arbitrarily restricting all causation to the relatively proximate cause of a phenomenon. Clearly that restriction is inappropriate; for example, it would be absurd for the defense attorney to argue that the defendant's intentionally firing a bullet into the victim's skull was *not* the cause of the victim's death on the grounds that the death certificate identifies the cause of death as that bullet's entering the victim's brain. But *sometimes* the relatively proximate cause *does* suffice to explain why something happened; for example, it makes perfect sense to attribute the victim's death to the defendant's intentionally firing a bullet into the victim's skull even though this would not have happened if firearms had never been invented.

Just so, when I wield Occam's razor to lop off morality from our moral beliefs. etc., I am not slicing at things willy-nilly but within a specific context where this makes sense. But let me now concede that my having adduced Occam's Razor might itself benefit from a slash of the blade, for I was hoping to clarify my refutation of morality thereby and instead may only have obscured it. In what follows I will revert, therefore, to the basic argument to the best explanation and strive to show not only that Explanation No. 3 all by itself suffices to explain empirical morality but also that, *on independent grounds*, Explanations 1 and 2 are no help at all.

Explanation No. 1, that God is responsible for the existence of empirical morality, was pretty much demolished by Socrates (i.e., Plato) in the *Euthyphro*. And in characteristic fashion, the pug-nosed one pulled off this feat by asking a question. The priest Euthyphro had been defending the claim that the right or "pious" thing to do is that which the gods (of Olympus) love. Socrates denied this. His first refutation was that, according to the stories about the gods, different gods love different and conflicting things; so how could their preferences answer our moral questions? But supposing all the gods loved the same things, or that there were just one God or at any rate one wisest and most just god (whom Socrates identified as Zeus), there would still be a question about the source of right and wrong: Do the gods love something because it is pious, or is something pious because the gods love it? Explanation No. 1 presumes the second disjunct, that something is pious or morally right because the gods love it. But the first, that the gods love something because it is right, is more acceptable to common sense or moral intuition.

The implicit reasoning behind this intuition is that we love and respect the gods because they are good, but this love and respect of ours for the gods would only make sense if we believed the gods were good precisely because they in turn loved what was good or morally right. Otherwise our attributing goodness to them would have no basis, and hence why would we spontaneously love and respect them? But this implies that the good and the right must be understood apart from divinity, for we judge divinity in light of them and not vice versa.

This brings us, then, to Explanation No. 2: Empirical morality owes its existence to our intuiting something inherent to the universe itself. This component or feature of the universe would be the secular metaphysical morality I characterized in Chapter 1. So just as e=mc^2 is true of the universe, so also is, say, Kant's categorical imperative: Never treat any person merely as a means. The problem with this explanation, however, is twofold. First, there is still lacking an adequate conceptualization of this metaphysical morality. In Chapter 1 I did not worry much about that because I was only trying to characterize how we normally think about morality, and I readily acknowledged that our notion of it is hazy if not downright confused. But now we can no longer rest content with this poor showing since metaphysical morality is in competition with an alternative and robust explanation of empirical morality, namely, Explanation No. 3. For that matter, even if there were no third explanation ready to hand, Explanation No. 2 could turn out to be just as insupportable as Explanation No. 1 has proven to be.

In fact, the failure of Explanation No. 1 is directly relevant to the prospects of Explanation No. 2, since the latter without the former seems to offer us commands without a commander.[12] This threatens to make Explanation No 2 not merely false but false because unintelligible. For thinking of morality as a kind of imperative—specifically, a categorical one, and more specifically, say, to never treat anyone merely as a means—was a way to understand morality's special nature. But if it no longer made sense to conceive metaphysical morality in this way, what alternative would there be? Recall again that a moral law is not like a law of nature, for the latter is not, strictly speaking, *obeyed*, but is more a description of what *will in fact* always occur (under the specified circumstances). A moral law, by contrast, is very definitely something to be *obeyed*—as we say: One *ought* always to do it (under the specified circumstances)—for otherwise it will *not* take effect. Yet what model do we have of such a thing if not a command from a commander?

It is for this very reason that some religious people insist that "Without God, nothing is prohibited."[13] No commander, no commands; hence, no God, then no "Thou shalt not" murder, steal, rape, etc. I think this is correct, even though I am not religious or at least not theistic. I have dubbed the principle "hard atheism," which holds that atheism implies amorality.[14] However, two implications that most theistic hard atheists[15] hold, I deny.

First (and as I will argue at length in Chapter 3), I do not believe that people would *in fact commit* more mayhem than they currently do if they ceased to believe in morality. Second, I do not believe that "*with*" God, anything is morally prohibited either.

For one thing, it would be simply fallacious to infer from the truth of hard atheism to the latter conclusion. Compare: From the truth of "If I am not wearing footwear, then I am not wearing sneakers" it does not follow that "If I *am* wearing footwear, then I *am* wearing sneakers." I might still not be wearing sneakers, but boots. Just so: From "No God, therefore no prohibitions" it does not follow that "With God, prohibitions." There might still not be any prohibitions. Compare another: "No God, then no four-sided triangles"; but even if there were a God, presumably there would still not be any four-sided triangles. Well, metaphysical morality is beginning to look more and more like a four-sided triangle: commands without a commander.

The second problem with Explanation No. 2 is that it has no story to tell, that is, no alternative to the commanderless commands. We might say: There is no *theory* of metaphysical morality. This is not in itself fatal, since we do accept that there are such things as "brute facts." But, again, in light of there being competition from an Explanation No. 3, which does indeed tell a story, Explanation No. 2 doesn't seem to have much to offer on which to base the claim of being the *best* explanation. Thus, when I consider my own reasons for believing in the Kantian categorical imperative to treat all persons as ends and not simply as means, all I can really say is that "it is obvious" as an appeal to my intuition. This also puts an intuitionist at the (obvious!) disadvantage of having no reply to anyone who does not share his or her intuition, or even has an opposing one.[16]

But I must immediately clarify what I mean by saying there is no story, for it is easy enough to concoct a fairy tale about anything. So by a story I mean an account that plausibly connects to the rest of reality. The saga of Santa Claus (to explain the appearance of gifts on Christmas morning) fails this test for the very reasons that cause us to disbelieve it as we mature. Reindeer don't fly. Nobody can visit every family on Earth in a single worldwide night, not to mention carry that many toys in a sleigh. Etc. No matter how much the details of a story may cohere with one another—and of course there have been entire worlds of fantasy elaborately constructed by the human imagination—if they do not also jibe with our most informed and reflective understanding of the world we live in, the story cannot be taken literally as an actual explanation.

My claim, then, is that there are no stories about metaphysical morality *other than self-contained ones whose connection to the rest of our beliefs about reality is tenuous.* Thus, note, stories *have* been told by ethicists about the nature of morality, but they are fantastical stories. The example par excellence is surely Immanuel Kant's Kingdom of Ends.[17] This is a realm where perfectly rational beings choose their own laws that shall thenceforth govern them as perfectly free beings. It is an exquisite and ingenious conception of morality as self-legislated law(s). It seems to have everything tied up as neatly as a Christmas gift from Martha Stewart, if not Santa Claus. Alas, however, it trades on a metaphysical figment, namely, a "noumenal" realm of free beings.[18] These free beings are none other than ourselves, who are able to initiate or *will* actions independently of the causal forces that influence us in the natural world. However, we only know ourselves as "phenomenal" beings in a cause-and-effect world. This is because our very ability to know is conditioned by a cause-and-effect structure: a kind of causal goggles or prescription lenses, as it were, through which we peer at reality, including ourselves, and without which we see nothing but a blur.[19]

What makes this an inadequate story about morality is that its postulation is only hypothetical or "transcendental."[20] Perhaps Kant's reasoning is correct, that noumenal freedom is necessary *if* morality is to exist. But it would then quite beg the question to conclude from this argument that this story is *true*: that pure freedom (and hence also metaphysical morality) does in fact exist. The mere fact that this story would explain *empirical* morality if the story *were* true is hardly an argument for its *being* true, since the whole point of the present exercise is to come up with a *plausible* story (indeed, the most plausible) for a phenomenon (viz., empirical morality) that could be explained by any number of stories, most of which are false. The question is, therefore: Have we any grounds for accepting *this* story as *plausible* (or more plausible than an alternative)? In other words, does a noumenal realm of freedom *connect up* (or connect up *better than* any alternative explanation) with the world as we know it in everyday experience and/or science?

My answer is "No." The full answer of course awaits the discussion of Explanation No. 3 as the purported *better* explanation. But more generally I will say this: The conception of a noumenal realm of reality, in which we are metaphysically free, somehow coexisting with a phenomenal realm of "appearance," in which we are causally determined, is just another example of the dualism that pervades traditional philosophic thinking.[21] Other prominent instances are mind and body, God and Creation, self and external world, value and fact. My verdict on the lot of them is skepticism about the first member of each pair. What seems most plausible to me now is that this kind of duality is pervasive, among philosophers and laypersons alike, because we crave an alternative to the mundane, i.e., to the second members of those pairs: body, Creation (the universe), the external world (the physical world), fact, and deterministic causality. (There is in turn an explanation of why we have this craving, for example, because *life*—that is, life in a physical body in a physical universe subject to the contingencies of brute fact and causality—*is hard*.) Most ironically and extraordinarily, then, humanity has conspired to designate as most real that which is in fact the dream: that stupendous metaphysical Reality "beneath" or "behind" or "beyond" "the appearances" (of body, etc.).

I do not mean to deny that appearance-and-reality is a useful metaphor, nor even that there is something like it in a fairly literal sense; for example, very often things are not as they appear, and science for one is adept at revealing realities that fly in the face of common sense and experience. What makes this real duality different from the philosophic one, however, is that in the former, the postulated reality and appearance *combine in a coherent picture* of (or story about) the world (however esoterically and theoretically mediated). The duality of noumena and phenomena, by contrast, is stark, and insofar as the twain ever "meet," it is by hocus-pocus fiat, as when Descartes declared the bridge between mind and body to be the pineal gland.[22] Of course here I am only reproducing on a wider scale the more particular complaint I have just lodged against metaphysical morality.

I should add, however, that there is also a mundane interpretation of Kant's Kingdom of Ends, which would sidestep the above objection. According to Kant[23] there is a test everyday reason can perform that will determine the moral: Simply try to imagine if your intended action could be brought about by a law of nature. If it could not, then the action would be wrong. For example, if you intended to lie to someone for personal benefit, imagine that it were a law of nature that anyone seeking to benefit from lying to someone else would, other things equal, do so—just as surely as someone jumping from a tenth-story window will, under specified conditions, fall at 32 feet per second per second. Kant argued that a practical contradiction would result, since in such a world this very kind of lie would defeat its own purpose by encountering universal skepticism—just as does anyone's urging you to avoid the delay of using a staircase by jumping from the tenth-story window. Thus, it looks like nature herself explains morality and reveals her mandates to us by our rational ability to detect contradiction.[24]

Unfortunately this version of Kant's story seems simply not to work. For one thing it presumes universal accord on just what our moral intuitions are, but that is problematical to say the least. For example, Kant himself is notorious for ruling out lying even in the case of trying to mislead a madman with a hatchet who is in hot pursuit of your innocent friend.[25] But even if we found some way to reconcile all of our moral intuitions, it is not at all clear that they would match the results of our reasoning even under Kant's stipulated conditions. Thus, when in moral mode I would consider it wrong to lie solely for trivial personal advantage at great cost to the person being lied to. Yet if everyone always lied under such circumstances, the lying would not necessarily fail. This is because everyone would, presumably, tell the truth when it was to their advantage to do so; so the net result would be that on any given occasion, one's auditor would only know that you might be lying or you might be telling the truth. But this is already the case in our actual world, and it does not seem to inhibit or otherwise defeat the common practice of lying by one iota.[26] The trick is still to figure out if it is to someone's advantage to lie, a problem for the real world as much as for Kant's imaginary world.[27]

Therefore the task has not been accomplished of accounting for the phenomena of morality (i.e., empirical morality) on the basis of morality (i.e., metaphysical morality), no matter whether the latter is understood as inherent in the world (*a là* Explanation No. 2) or as divine (*a là* Explanation No. 1). What remains, then, is to see whether empirical morality can be explained without reference to morality. That is what Explanation No. 3 endeavors to do. But the sufficiency of Explanation No. 3 to pull this off is hardly in dispute. For not only is there an overabundance of plausible stories to tell about why we feel, believe, and act as we do with respect to morality, but also, the proponents of the two other explanations will generally accept them.[28] The point of contention has only been whether our everyday beliefs and assumptions about morality *are true*, and hence our feelings and attitudes and behaviors that are based on those beliefs *justified by them*. Absent metaphysical morality, they are not. Hence, by the logic of inference to the best explanation, the case has, I think, been made: We have a better way to account for our experience of morality than to postulate the existence of morality, so morality does not exist (or at least it would be irrational to believe that it does).

I admit that that was a bit too swift, so let me say more. First of all, the logic of the argument needs tightening up. The nonexistence of morality would not follow unless it had also been shown that morality is not needed to explain *anything else* either. But this logical gap can be easily plugged by means of the following assumption: If metaphysical morality is not needed to explain empirical morality, then it is not needed to explain anything else either. After all, we do not expect to see morality cropping up in our theory of the physical world, do we? Oh, I suppose that is not a merely rhetorical question in the wacky world of philosophy. For example, Leibniz was notorious for attributing the existence of the world not only to God's power and knowledge but also to God's goodness, this being "the best of all possible worlds."[29] I am tempted simply to mock Leibniz's theodicy in the manner of Voltaire's *Candide*, but logically that would have no more purchase than Johnson's kicking of the stone to refute Berkeley's idealism.[30] I do at least suggest that the burden of proof rests on anyone who claimed that morality serves a necessary function in the best explanation of any feature of our world other than empirical morality.

A less theologically laden attempt has been to argue that *person* is an inherently moral concept, such that if there were no morality, there would be no persons.[31] Kant could be understood in this manner since, for him, a person is precisely that sort of entity that possesses moral considerability as an essential property.[32] But I submit that it is more natural to interpret this as a factual rather than a definitional affirmation. Thus, *person* can be defined independently of moral status, and then the additional claim is made that all such entities, in virtue of their defining characteristics, are worthy of moral consideration. That is, they *would be* if there were such a thing as morality. Therefore persons would be moral in the way lying is. Lying can be defined quite independently of whether it is right or wrong or even something that is subject to that type of assessment. For example, lying could plausibly be defined as making a verbal expression that one intends to be understood as true even though one believes it to be false. It is a completely separate question whether that is wrong to do, always or sometimes, or, more to the point, whether that sort of judgment is even applicable to it. After all, the readers of this book do not believe that lying is assessable by whether Santa Claus judges it naughty or nice, or by whether Zeus loves it; similarly, lying is lying even if not assessable by whether it is morally right or wrong.

Let me now try to do an end run around all such attempts to defend the necessity of morality to our understanding of the world, by laying out my own (modest?) understanding of the universe and of how we come to have that understanding. There is spacetime, and then there is what spacetime contains.[33] Among the latter are physical objects, such as dust particles, stars, and planets. A distinct subset of physical objects are biological organisms. Human beings are one type of biological organism. We humans relate to one another in ways that conform to various sorts of lawful description, which are studied by sciences like sociology and anthropology. Our behavior as individuals is also studied by psychology, economics, neuroscience, evolutionary psychology, cognitive science, and so on. None of these sciences makes essential reference to metaphysical morality in its explanations or theories.[34] Nothing in human experience cannot in theory be explained by these theories, including the false beliefs that most human beings have about the universe.

The (claimed) false belief that is most relevant to the present inquiry is, of course, that morality exists. How can this belief be accounted for if it is false? Let me count the ways.[35] The general point is that the belief (and its attendant feelings and behaviors) performs a function in the scheme of things that tends to preserve that belief. For example, a population that contained human beings who were ready to put group welfare ahead of their personal welfare would seem more likely to thrive than one that did not contain such individuals. Therefore we could expect to see extant societies promoting the virtue of self-sacrifice by inculcating this motive in its young and rewarding those who exhibited it at any point in their life. One way of inculcating the motive would be to teach and preach the existence of an overriding, absolute, universal, objective, metaphysical (and usually divine) demand for self-sacrifice.[36] And this demand we call morality.[37]

3 Would Amorality Be Viable?

I will take it as having been established that morality, that is, metaphysical morality, does not exist. The argument was, in essence, that *empirical* morality can be accounted for without the postulation of (metaphysical) morality, and, over and above that merely Occamistic consideration, empirical morality can be accounted for *more plausibly* without, than by, postulating (metaphysical) morality. But the amoralism I wish to defend in this book goes beyond the claim that (metaphysical) morality does not exist to include as well the claim that empirical morality, although surely existent, is dispensable (and, indeed, with good riddance, which I shall argue in the next chapter). In other words, not only does morality not exist, but the *belief* in morality serves no essential purpose in human affairs. So the amoralist need not end up in the awkward position of perpetrating a Noble Lie[1] but can advocate a thoroughgoing amoralism[2] in both theory and practice.

Think of how people felt, behaved, and spoke when they believed that the earth was flat; the falsity of their fundamental assumption did not seem to matter much to their daily lives. Consistently with that, not much needed to change when people did become convinced that the earth is spherical . . . not to mention, rotating on an axis . . . and revolving around the sun . . . and whizzing around the outskirts of the Milky Way Galaxy . . . and heading for a collision with the Andromeda Galaxy . . . and growing ever more distant from most of the other galaxies in the universe. Life pretty much goes on as before. I believe this would be the case, *mutatis mutandis*, if an amoral regime were to replace our present, moralist one.

Normally, however, people believe that life would not go on as before. Amorality is viewed by moralists as a potential scourge. By a *moralist* I mean someone who believes there is such a thing as morality (in the metaphysical sense of Chapter 1); hence an amoralist is one who denies this. But an amoralist could also be something more than this, namely, a person who actually lives as if there were no such thing as morality. What adjustments (if any) would the full-blown amoralist need to make in transitioning from moralism? We can even ask: Would the mere conviction that morality does not exist likely bring about certain changes in a person's other beliefs and attendant feelings, behaviors, and utterances? Finally, we could inquire about the effect on an entire society were amoralism to become a pervasive doctrine. Many people fear that this could be the ultimate human catastrophe, short of another extinction-level impact by an asteroid or comet. There might be instant and universal mayhem.

But while I agree that a counter-conversion[3] to amorality is likely to have some effects, I believe that they would be in the main benign, and in any event not catastrophic. In this chapter I will argue for the moderate conclusion that things would not get worse. In the next chapter I will argue that they might get a lot better. What I need to do is characterize what an amoral life and world would be like. Let me give a label to my positive thesis: desirism. For an amoralist there is no moral "should." So what is there? My answer is, in a word, desire. An amoralist wants to know not what he or she should do (nor what is good), but what he or she wants to do (or the way he or she wants the world to be).

Now, as simple-sounding as this claim is, it is actually exceedingly tricky to tease apart; for depending on how you interpret it, it could easily come out either true or false. If wanting (desiring) something is the same as being motivated to achieve or acquire it, then desirism seems to be asserting a trivial or *analytic* truth. What we do is always an action, and an action is always motivated, and another name for motivation is "desire." Thus, even a moralist who always strove consciously to do the right thing, even when this meant acting in opposition to other things she would much rather be doing, would, in the last analysis, be doing what she wanted to do, simply in virtue of being motivated to do the right thing.

On the other hand, if "desire" referred to a particular kind of mental disposition or *inclination*, then desirism would appear to be false of the actual world by the same consideration, namely, that sometimes we do act contrary to our desires.[4] "I really wanted to take that watch, but I know it's wrong to steal, so I didn't." Of course it could still be my thesis that an *amoral* world would be desirist in this sense, since the whole point would be *not* to act contrary to one's desires, that is, in the inclinational sense of "desire."

What is the world supposed to be like that permits us to act *contrary* to desire? Immanuel Kant gave us one picture. Our behavior is motivated by a special faculty of *will*, which is capable of responding to the dictates of our conscience, which in turn "channels" or intuits the dictates of metaphysical morality.[5] Note that this is supposed to be always the case. Thus, even when we do something that we desire in the inclinational sense, we do it not because of the desire but because we *will* to act in accordance with that desire.

The desirist scheme I have in mind would not permit such a thing for the metaphysical reason that there is only a natural world of causality, into which there can be no moral intervention from a supernatural or "noumenal" realm, no more than there could be intervention by Jehovah or Zeus. Actions are little miracles on the moralist scheme, for they interrupt or at least bypass the causal flow. Our will is therefore *free* precisely because it can (and always does) function flexibly in response to any and all natural influences. The will is not, as we say, *determined* by anything in, or even outside of nature.[6]

But desirism is precisely the denial of this possibility; thus desirism is a metaphysical claim about the scope of human (or animal) motivation, namely, that it is restricted to the realm of natural causality, and more particularly, to the influence of mental attitudes that we are used to call "desire." Therefore the amoralist or desirist parsing of your acting "*contrary* to desire" is simply that *another* desire, or set of desires, caused you to do *that*. For example, you took a cold shower when there was no hot water even though "I *really* don't want to!" not because you exerted your will to act contrary to your desires but because you wanted *even more* to be fresh as a daisy for your date.

For all that, however, "desire" remains ambiguous if not obscure.[7] For one thing a desire could be either intrinsic or extrinsic. Thus, I might be motivated to go for a walk because I wanted to lose weight, so my desire to go for a walk had its source in another desire, which was "external" to the immediate one; alternatively I might be motivated simply by the desire to go for a walk. Another distinction of desire is between first-order and second-order desires. I may have a desire to smoke and also a desire not to desire to smoke. All of these sorts of desire are part of the mix of what I mean by desire in the context of desirism. Thus, sometimes desire in my sense will denote a motivation, which itself consists of another desire in conjunction with a belief; for example, I desire to go for a walk = I desire to lose weight + I believe that going for walks reduces weight. The component desire could itself be intrinsic or "basic": "I just want to be thinner, that's all!" Or it could itself be another motivation: I desire to lose weight = I desire to be popular + I believe that thinner people are more popular. And so forth.

According to desirism, therefore, even when a moralist is "doing the right thing," all that is going on is that she is being motivated by ordinary desires, whose etiology is none other than the mechanism of the world. Any "will" she is exercising would be nothing but a subset of these, having no access to, not to mention being influenced by, something supernatural. Therefore desirism claims what is a truism only for the naturalist, namely, that our actions or intentional behaviors are always motivated by some desire or other; but this is a significant assertion, because moralists implicitly believe to the contrary, namely, that our actions are always motivated by a faculty of will that is distinct from and not in any way determined by desire in the "inclinational" sense that desirism picks out. Part of a moralist's motivation could indeed be her *belief* in a supernatural realm. But then her motivation would contain a false belief. There would be nothing out of the ordinary about *that*. It happens to us all the time and does not require the postulation of a supernatural realm to explain it.

So suppose that you were rushing along a woodland path to get back to your car because you wanted very much to arrive at an important meeting on time, but then you noticed a little girl floundering in the stream that runs alongside the path. You would much rather keep on your way than risk delay to rescue the child and also have to return home to change out of your wet clothes. But it is easy enough to imagine that you also had an even stronger desire to do your moral duty; and so you were sufficiently motivated to overcome your preference to continue on your way and rescue the child. What would happen, then, if we replaced the delusions of the moralist with the clear-eyed amoralism of the desirist? Would he (or you) simply ignore the drowning child and continue on his way to his meeting? Not necessarily, and I would claim, not even likely so. For there is an abundance of desires that could motivate the same action as the moral desire. And even more to the point: There is an abundance of alternative desires or motivations that, unlike the moral desire, involve only *belief*-components that are *true* (or at least rational). Here is a partial list:

Fear: You are more afraid of the possibility of being arrested and reviled for leaving the child to her fate if someone should happen to see you, or the child herself survive to tell the tale, than you are desirous of arriving at your meeting on time.

Greed and selfishness: You are more moved by the thoughts that the child's parents will be your friends for life and want to reward you and that you will achieve fame as a local hero if you rescue the child than you are desirous of arriving at your meeting on time.

Boredom: You are more moved by the unexpected opportunity to do something outside the humdrum habits and priorities of your everyday existence than you are to arrive at your meeting on time.

Compassion: You are simply moved by the plight of the child more than you are to arrive at your meeting on time.

Self-concept: You are more moved by the image of yourself as compassionate than by your desire to arrive at the meeting on time.

Idealism: You are more moved by an image of a world that contains selfless deeds than you are by your desire to arrive at the meeting on time.

I would even make the further claim that most of the time that we do something "moral" it is in fact for one or more of the above reasons rather than the moral one.[8] Morality (that is, its agents) may come along after the fact to approve what we have done and even take the credit for it; but morality is not why we did it. And that is one of my arguments for why an avowedly amoral world would likely be just as viable as the currently avowedly moral one. But my main argument is that the morally right action is typically overdetermined by nonmoral as well as moral considerations.

Here is an analogy. We all know that we are going to die. Yet it is arguable that we live as if we were going to live forever, or at least *would* live forever if we were careful to avoid accidents and had consistent good luck; in other words, we live from day to day as if death were not inevitable but only a possibility. The explanation is simple: For most of us it is an unpleasant thought, so we put it out of our minds, and furthermore it does not seem particularly relevant to most of what we do and need to attend to. Just so, I am suggesting, morality: Most of us believe in it, but it is only in the background, along with the thought of our mortality. Our day to day lives are filled with things we want to do or feel we must do, but our actions are largely governed by more immediate motives.

But are there not occasions when morality does become salient, namely, when it commands that we not do x, and nonmoral considerations urge that we do x? Well, perhaps. But here I would point out the chameleonic "virtues" of morality. I ask you, Dear Reader: Can you truly imagine any action whatsoever, no matter how heinous to your own sensibilities, that has not been upheld as, not only permissible but even virtuous by some moral scheme or other? Simply flick on the telly for all the proof you need. Still, you would probably insist (if you were a moralist) that those other moralities are simply false; your own moral sense or conscience is the True Guide to what is Right and what is Wrong. My reply: "That's what they all say."

Let me put it this way. It seems fairly obvious to me that not only do people *always* do what they want to do, but also people *usually* believe that what they are doing is morally right or at least permissible. So I would not expect to find too much variance between the actions of people who do what they want and say so and the actions of others who do what they want but call it "right." Desire is the dog and morality is the tail, but we kid ourselves it's the other way around.[9] Morality is therefore chiefly our own stamp of approval on what we do for other reasons. And to the degree that it is not—to the degree that we do truly heed what we believe to be moral truth that runs contrary to our other motives—to that degree, I would say, we are at least as likely to make trouble for ourselves and others as not,[10] so at best it's a wash.

But, yes, there do seem to be occasions when we act in ways that we ourselves believe are morally wrong,[11] and we may (or may not) genuinely repent afterward. This hardly counts against amorality, however, for it only shows the degree of morality's ineffectualness. So when morality is not simply an empty honorific applied to what we would do anyway, it may be that morality is honored mainly in the breach. Look around the world as we know it, in days past and today, filled with every kind of horror intentionally inflicted by human beings on one another and other animals: Whether it is done in morality's name or in admitted violation thereof, can we easily imagine a world that would be even worse by the moralist's lights? Indeed, I am amused and amazed when a moralist lodges this kind of complaint against amorality, for it strikes me as the very paradigm of the pot calling the kettle black. Therefore I believe there would be little to fear from an alternative regime by comparison.

Yet there is the nagging doubt that something critically important to our well-being, such as it is, or even our viability is at stake in the question of morality's hold on us (that is, the hold of the *belief* in morality). So that even if morality were a figment, some Noble Lie would be well advised. In this Darwinian age it is not enough to say that the false belief in and veneration of morality are due to ignorance and superstition (or whatever); we are obliged also to explain why such ignorance and superstition have been sustained by the conditions of our existence.[12] For if they did not serve some vital function, they would, presumably, have been winnowed out . . . unless they were so insignificant as to slip between the cracks. But it is not likely that a phenomenon so prominent as empirical morality has gone unnoticed by the competitive forces of survival. If it did not give us some advantage, it would not be so integral a part of our lives. Therefore we dare not blithely assume that its elimination would have no detrimental, even fatal effect on human prospects. As the sad history of missionary colonialism has shown, barging in to "fix" specific things can have disastrous long-term consequences for a whole society. So conservatism is not in itself unreasonable.

But do we therefore adopt a hands-off policy regarding the status quo, lest some present improvement set in motion a catastrophe for ourselves down the road? To think so without some specific evidence or argument for believing it strikes me as mere superstition—like "If man was meant to fly. . . ." Furthermore, a clear understanding of how natural selection functions reveals that it is quite myopic; today's adaptive feature could doom us tomorrow, since the environment in which we must "survive" is forever changing. Furthermore, survival is not necessarily equivalent to well-being. Thus, might not more human beings be happy today—and humanity itself have a better outlook of continuing at all—if there were fewer of us? So a morality of "Be fruitful and multiply," which enshrines procreative marriage and proscribes abortion and euthanasia, could have outlived its usefulness. Similarly, despite (or even *because of*) humanity's numerical thriving, there may be reasons for frowning upon the retention of morality as such, even if we owe our current superabundance to it.

One important observation relevant to the question of how amorality would shape up in comparison to morality as a guide to life (i.e., as an ethics) is that desirism is not the same as egoism. To maintain that all motivation consists in desire, whether intrinsic or extrinsic, simple or componential, is not at all to hold that we are motivated only by self-interest, however enlightened or unenlightened. In my list of nonmoral motives above, at least half of them had no obvious connection to personal welfare. We could also add love and caring to compassion, idealism, etc., as common motives that are not necessarily self-directed, that is, directed towards oneself, although of course they emanate from oneself.[13] So while some individual desirist could indeed be a thoroughgoing egoist, another could be a total altruist, and everything in between or at right angles. Insofar, then, as non-egoistic motivation is a prerequisite of human survival, we need not conclude that amorality would necessarily be fatal.

Indeed, an amoralist could even retain erstwhile-moral values. For example, even though I espouse amorality, I myself continue to be Kantian in my view of most if not all human action. Thus, I look upon the "mere use" of one human being by another—in a word, exploitation—as distasteful, so I strive to avoid engaging in it myself, recoil at being so used by another, and look with disfavor on anyone else treating someone in that way. But I also strive to hold this attitude in a nonmoralist way. Admittedly this is, emotionally speaking, like threading a needle, but the distinction is real. For example, I wish to avoid being *offended* by exploitation, for that would imply a moral assessment of exploitation as (morally) *wrong*. I do not believe that there is any such thing as *wrong* in this sense, regarding exploitation or anything else. In other words, exploitation does not have such a property. Rather, exploitation has the property of eliciting from me (but maybe not from others) a reaction of displeasure (of a certain kind). I intensely dislike exploitation. I want it to stop. I am motivated to strive to eliminate it from the world. That could also be the case if I thought exploitation were morally wrong, but then there would be something *in addition* constituting my attitude, namely, the belief in an external or objective endorsement by the cosmos or God. This I can no longer countenance because it is a fairy tale.[14]

I can even see a possible *advantage* to amorality as a vehicle for moral-like reasoning. Take the philosophy of utilitarianism: It has been subjected to unrelenting criticism since its formal inception by Bentham and Mill, including by me.[15] In Chapter 1 I relented somewhat and allowed it as a sometime alternative to Kantianism, my favored theory of morality. But even so I could not have meant it in its literal sense of endorsing acts that maximize happiness, because, by my earlier arguments elsewhere, such a conception is utter nonsense.[16] However, as an amoralist I am free to apply utilitarian-like thinking in an everyday way *just because I want to* or find it useful for my own purposes. Thus, if Kantianism told me I must not lie to the Nazi soldier at my door about the whereabouts of the Frank family, who are hidden in my attic, because I would be treating the soldier merely as a means to my own ends of self- and other-protection, I could quite easily yield to the utilitarian thought that it's better overall that I do so in this instance. However, I would not be employing literal utilitarianism here, for, for all I know, a surviving member of the Frank family may go on to parent the great-great-great-grandmother of a malevolent dictator who destroys the whole world. (But—who knows?—that might be a better outcome relative to what would have transpired in the universe had that fiendish fellow *not* destroyed the whole world, i.e., Earth. And so on ad inf.) In other words, all that we may really care about are short-term or *foreseeable* consequences of our and others' behavior. But these would not ground a literal or moral utilitarianism because they bear no knowable relation to the actual (i.e., long-term) consequences of the behavior in question. Therefore a "faux" or nonmoral version of utilitarianism (or any other moralist philosophy) might suffice as a "guide to life" or ethics even though moralist utilitarianism is hopeless.

But now another worry arises for the claim of amorality's viability as an ethics—as a reliable guide to life, as a practical philosophy for an individual or a society. I have acknowledged that I remain somewhat of a Kantian in my outlook and motivation, despite having rejected Kantianism as a morality (because I reject morality as such). Let us suppose this is conceptually coherent and even psychologically possible (both of which I believe it is). Is it not fairly obvious, however, that it might have been otherwise, that is, that I might not be, and never had been, a Kantian? I surely grant this. It does not require much straining of the brain to explain why I did gravitate to Kantianism in the first place. A biographical sketch would reveal the relevant tendencies in my personality and the relevant background in my upbringing, education, and so forth. Or even if there were some inevitability about it in my case, I must allow that an analogous inevitability could have produced an anti-Kantianism in somebody else—somebody who did not mind or who positively reveled in exploitation.

The worry, then, is this: If a viable life or society depends on having a healthy dose of Kantian motivation, but Kantian motivation is purely contingent or "accidental," then the conscious rejection of morality cannot guarantee viability. In fact the worry is even stronger than that, for the amoral individual or society will actively spurn the sort of indoctrination that leads to Kantianism or any other moralist philosophy.[17] One would *tsk tsk* the roots of one's own Kantianism as nothing but the vestige of a misguided upbringing, and avoid reproducing it in one's own offspring. But insofar as one were successful in counteracting one's own atavistic tendencies and in preventing anything like them from taking hold in the first place in one's children, what would be left to take their place? Can one be sure that the resultant citizens would have a negative attitude towards exploitation, or at least one as strong as mine still is? What grounds are there for thinking so?

But I have already given my answer: There are motives aplenty other than moralist ones for many of the attitudes and behaviors that morality would endorse. One reason is trivial: Morality is capable of endorsing anything at all. But even taking the substantive account of morality I gave in Chapter 1 as a kind of Kantianism, there is much redundancy within the human heart and mind. Again: I suspect that our desires or "feelings" have led the way all along (due ultimately to evolutionary pressures), with morality arriving later on the scene to spur us on with divine or mythic encouragement. I do think the Dennettian worry[18] remains: that this "mythic spurring on" might itself provide humanity with some sort of selective advantage. But, again, this should only induce caution and conscientiousness in our assessment of empirical morality's continued utility in light of modern conditions.[19] It does not mean that we should simply acquiesce in morality's ongoing predominance in human affairs.[20]

4 Might Amorality Be Preferable?

Chapter 3 concluded that an amoral life or society or "world" would at least be viable, and, further, at least as viable as the present world. But that is hardly enough to warrant our going to the trouble of changing everything, including some of our most basic assumptions and ways of speaking and thinking, only to end up in the same practical place.[1] Thus, we want to know whether there might plausibly be some *advantage* to an amoral regime. Let me say at once that one obvious advantage is that our beliefs about the world would be, as per Chapter 2, more (quantitatively and qualitatively) *true*. For is not truth something that we value for its own sake?

This still might not be viewed as an advantage, however, or a *relative* advantage (over the present, moralist world). For we will have lost something too, namely, a certain kind of reason for what we do; and this reason is something we are used to treasuring. The reason (or one way of putting it) is that people have *moral worth*, and hence *moral rights*. We like to think that we ourselves have certain "unalienable" prerogatives and immunities simply in virtue of being a person; and the same rights of others are what ground our moral obligations to them—to do unto them or to refrain from doing unto them.[2] The amoralist substitute of *desire* does not replace this worth, nor does it *require* anything of us; so even if desire served practically to motivate roughly the same behavior towards others, it would do so on a very different basis. If we desired to help somebody else, or not harm them, even intrinsically, but not for any *moral* reason, we would only be, as it were, bestowing a gift on them; there would be nothing *"in" them* that made our solicitous attitude objectively appropriate, not to mention requisite (or in *ourselves* that warranted others' like treatment of *us*).

So the gain of truth from embracing amorality, intrinsically valuable though truth may be, could be offset by the felt loss of (belief in) moral worth. But now this raises a further question, or really a prior question that was skipped over in the preceding chapter: What place would intrinsic value have in the brave new world of amorality? By *value* I mean what we also refer to as *good*.[3] For example, if you think that health is good, then health could be said to be a value of yours, something that you value. People value all sorts of things, and not always the same or even compatible things. Some people value peace, while others value war; and in Ecclesiastes fashion, some of us value both, each in its time. Of course it is not the same to recognize war as sometimes a regrettable necessity and to think that war is a good or valued thing. So perhaps the way to think about value is that it attaches especially to that which we *desire intrinsically*. Thus, a certain type of warrior personality may truly love war for its own sake and hence be said to value war unambiguously. On the other hand, even someone who felt that war served only an instrumental purpose, such as to build character, might view war as good for that reason, and hence value it. So there are shades and distinctions about our use of the notion of value. What remains constant, however, is that value is subjective.

But have I not referred to things that have value in themselves? That does not sound like something subjective. My answer is that it is easy to confuse two quite different attributes. What I do allow and maintain is that human beings (and other animals) are capable of valuing things "for their own sake." Examples: going for a walk just because you like going for a walk; loving your child "just for himself," such that you desire only his welfare, even at genuine cost to yourself. However, this is quite distinct from the metaphysical notion that your child and your going for a walk have *inherent* value. The latter notion locates value in the entity or event itself. What I have called intrinsic value, by contrast, means only that you or someone values someone or something for no reason of utility but only for its own qualities. Thus: You love your child for his own sake (and not simply because he can take out the garbage for you), but *I* might think that your boy is a brat and take no joy in his presence or even well-being. These are perfectly compatible valuations because they are subjective. However, an objectivist about values could maintain *in addition* that your child has *inherent* value—simply in virtue of being a person or being a living being or being a rational being or what have you.

What has only been implicit so far—in my arguments for both the non-existence of metaphysical morality and the recommended elimination of empirical morality—is that I also mean to impugn objective value. The reason that sort of valuation is implicated in my brief against morality is that it is quite natural to ground *moral* value, such as the rightness or wrongness of an action, in inherent value. Suppose your child (and mine and everybody else's, not to mention we ourselves) had inherent value. Then if anyone were to treat your child in a way that ignored that metaphysical fact, he or she would be doing something *morally wrong*. For example, if I were to bully your child because I did not like him, I would be acting *immorally* because bullying manifests a failure to appreciate the inherent value of all persons. That is the kind of story that could be told, anyway. We might quibble about the details, such as which things or beings have inherent value and "how much"; but the basic idea is that certain components of the universe possess value inherently and thereby ground our proper behavior towards them.

Yet another way to illustrate the difference between intrinsic and inherent value is to show how they could be in conflict with each other. So suppose I did *not* bully your child but treated him with kindness and respect whenever I met him; this could be so even though I found him disagreeable and avoided him whenever discreetly possible. Thus, I could be said to be behaving morally in view of your child's inherent value as a person, while nonetheless placing no intrinsic value on him. Well, one reason I am an amoralist is that inherent value has as little place in the best explanation of the universe that is known to me as does metaphysical morality itself. In fact these "two" could amount to the same thing, depending on one's *moral* metaphysics. The kind of moral metaphysics I dispensed with in Chapter 2 postulated *commands* coming from either a divinity or some feature of the universe itself. Inherent values could be seen as refining or supplementing those pictures or stories. Specifically, the inherent values of things in the universe (or perhaps even of the universe as such) could be precisely what constitute the "commanding feature" of the universe. So "the universe commands that I never treat anybody merely as a means" would turn out to be a less precise way of saying that all persons have inherent value, which is a property that requires fundamental respect for anything that possesses it.

I have already argued in Chapter 3 that I could still have plenty of good reasons for not bullying your son even absent morality, and here I reaffirm that that is so, even absent your son's having any inherent value. Again: I view inherent or objective value to be as mythical as morality, and they may amount to the same thing. But I raise the issue now because it could seem that by inquiring into the possible *advantages* of *an amoral regime*, I am implicitly relying on some notion of objective value or goodness. Indeed, this charge could have been brought against even the more modest claim of Chapter 3 that an amoral world would at least be *no worse* than the present world of presumably moral governance. I was able to ignore the issue there because I argued the point in terms of adequacy to preserve existing behaviors, without judging the preservation of existing behaviors as either a good thing or a bad thing. But in fact one could easily mean any one of three quite distinct claims in asserting the adequacy (or superiority) of an amoral regime:

1. An amoral regime would leave us with at least as much moral behavior—that is, behavior that a moralist would deem "moral" or morally right—as we have now (or more than we have now).
2. An amoral regime would be objectively at least as good as (or better than) the way things are now.
3. An amoral regime would leave us feeling at least as happy or satisfied as (or more so than) we currently do.

In the preceding chapter I only meant to be defending (1) . . . or at any rate the possibility of (1). I had and have no wish to defend (2). And in the present chapter I am examining the "better than" version of (3): call it Claim 3'. I could also put Claim 3' in the language of desirism, thus: If we came to live by the understanding that all of our intentional behavior is determined by our desires and not by any acts of a metaphysically free will in response to a metaphysically absolute morality, we would, other things equal, be happier or more satisfied with our lot because we preferred it, that is, liked it or desired it more than the rejected (and delusive) alternative.

Note, then: *It's desires all the way down.* For even the "intrinsic value" of *truth* (and in particular, the truth of amoralism) is subject to our desires, which are contingent and hence potentially variable and diverse. This does not make truth itself "relative," but it makes our *valuation* of truth relative to our desires. Thus, the earth may not be flat, but if it suited our preferences that it were, or we were merely indifferent, then the actual shape of the earth could take a back seat in our practical deliberations. A classic example of this type comes from Arthur Conan Doyle's *A Study in Scarlet* (ch. 2), when Sherlock Holmes expostulates to Dr. Watson:

> "What the deuce is it to me?" he interrupted impatiently; "you say that we go round the sun. If we went round the moon it would not make a pennyworth of difference to me or to my work."

My first claim in this chapter, however, was that, as a matter of fact human beings do by and large have a preference for believing what is true (or at least rational) rather than what is false (or irrational). Indeed, one reason it is difficult to find a counterexample is that the more patent the falsehood that a person ignores or even claims to believe, the more vehement, it often seems, will be their insistence that it is true or that it doesn't matter—a sign, I think, of inner struggle to overcome the preference for truth. At any rate, *to the degree* that we human beings do value truth, amorality would have the advantage over morality (if, of course, you accepted the argument of Chapter 2 for the truth of amorality).

But I will place more emphasis on other sorts of considerations, since I *am* willing to concede that our preference for truth over falsehood is only *prima facie* or "other things equal"; indeed in this respect it is very much like our preference for morality. In other words, both preferences or values are easily overwhelmed by other factors (albeit, as suggested in the preceding paragraphs, also highly "adaptable" or, to use the word from Chapter 3, chameleonic—thereby masking their weakness to overcome conflicting desires, even as they exert their strength to delude us into believing there is no conflict). So the question I now address is whether a clear-eyed review of the relative effects of believing and disbelieving in morality would move us to prefer an amoral regime, apart from the intrinsic value of believing what is true (or for that matter, apart from whether the belief in morality *is* true[4]). I believe that it would.

Might Amorality Be Preferable? 39

At first my position may seem to contradict an impression left by Chapter 3, which is that an amoral world would be largely indistinguishable from the present, moral world. So if we are now discounting the independent significance of truth, on what basis could an amoral world be preferred? But recall that the previous discussion pertained only to the *moral* adequacy of an amoral regime; in that respect, there may not be much to tell between them. Indeed, how could there be? For two reasons: (1) as noted, "morally right" can be and has been attributed to any and all types of actions, and (2) *ex hypothesi,* there is no moral truth of the matter to decide which attributions are correct! So in arguing the advantages of amorality as an ethics, I am not trying to out-moralize morality. The criterion of "better" in my claim is rather that, on reflection, you, the reader, will find empirical amorality more attractive and motivating than empirical morality.

But I must immediately draw yet another distinction, for what I introduced above as Claim 3′, viz., that an amoral regime would leave us feeling happier or more satisfied than we currently do, is *not* what I will defend. The reason I will not and *cannot* defend that claim is that *nobody* can confidently predict the future of life on Earth. One very general reason for this is that the question pertains to a single instance. This, I think, is the import of speaking of "natural *history*," as opposed to "earth *science.*" I understand *history* to refer to any story of unique events; this is in contradistinction to *science*, which looks for patterns or laws. While many laws may be presumed to impact upon and indeed determine the future of life on Earth, there is no set of laws that governs terrestrial life's destiny *as such*. Thus, just as the roll of a die is completely determined by the laws of nature plus existing conditions and yet, for all practical purposes is the epitome of random chance or "luck," other things equal (for example, the die is not biased), so the future of life on Earth is, other things equal (for example, no extinction-size cometary impact is known to be imminent), unpredictable.

A simpler argument is just to look at what we usually call "history." Take something as apparently benign as Jesus' ministry to "Love thy neighbor as thyself," this being "The entire law . . . summed up in a single command" (Galatians 5:14). What untold horrors this has visited on humanity (and other animals): the Crusades, the Inquisition, witch trials, anti-Semitism, the suppression and disparagement of scientific inquiry and achievement, the facilitation of colonialism, slavery, sexism, homophobia, war, factory farming, etc. Of course Jesus' words have also inspired countless acts of unabashed beneficence and enlightenment; even so, to call the net results a wash could strike many people as vastly optimistic. But the side of science is hardly better. We all know the main practical upshot of Einstein's eureka that $e=mc^2$: the two largest instantaneous holocausts in human history and the subsequent threat for at least a generation of imminent annihilation of the whole of humanity. Meanwhile, it is almost certain that you and I would never have existed if not for Hitler.[5] Insofar as we wish to judge the love commandment and Einstein's brilliance and our own existence as good things (i.e., things we like) and Hitler and witch trials and the nuclear arms race as evils (i.e., things we dislike), history seems not merely indifferent but sometimes positively perverse in her causal correlations between the two.[6] Therefore even if amorality turned out to be not only true (like e=mc^2) but an idea we found attractive (like the love commandment), it would not "follow" that its general adoption by the world, in all its flawed and lip-service reality, would result in a life or society we would prefer to the life or society that would have resulted had it not been adopted (or had it been adopted more faithfully, not to mention ideally). Such things are imponderable.

The distinction I wish to draw, therefore, is between the claim that an amoral regime would leave us (society, humanity) feeling happier or more satisfied than we currently do and the claim that on reflection (e.g., after reading this book), you, the reader, will find empirical amorality more attractive and motivating than empirical morality. The latter claim makes no long-term prediction about how things will turn out "in the end" (for you or society), so it is the one I will defend. However, I shall certainly feel myself at liberty to put forward considerations suggesting a rosy outcome for a world that embraced amoralism; and that thought would, naturally, form part of the appeal I claim for amorality. But even my more circumscribed claim (that you will find amorality appealing) is at base an empirical one, and therefore I, being a (non-experimental) philosopher, am ill-suited to support it with sufficient evidence. For example, I have not run any experiments to see if people exposed to the ideas in this monograph exhibited a positive change of attitude toward amorality.[7] In the final analysis, what I have to offer are the reasons *I myself* have found persuasive for switching allegiances . . . and even there I must acknowledge that I could be the last person to know what has *actually* moved me to become an amoralist.[8]

WHAT I DON'T LIKE ABOUT MORALITY

So without further ado, let me first identify various features of morality that I dislike, to wit:

Morality is angry. Morality is an emotionally fraught phenomenon.[9] There are many emotions that play moral roles, such as pity, compassion, shame, and guilt, but angry ones are prevalent and may even predominate. These include indignation, disgust, condemnation, outrage, contempt, and resentment. It can be truly astonishing and revelatory to discover how much rage is involved in one's own moral judgments. This, by the way, is a perfect example of how philosophy must sometimes be more (or less) than arguments (that is, the giving of logical reasons); for to be convinced of my claim about morality and anger one must really know one's own heart, and this is likely to come about only by means of prolonged meditation and introspection.[10]

I myself have become so sensitized to the morality-anger connection that I see it now as almost an identity. In other words, it is not only that being moral often, even typically, means being angry, but also that being angry means being moral. For when I consider myself being angry about something, I find that there is an implicit judgment that that about which or about whom I am angry is somehow (morally) wrong or bad. If this were not the case, then on a belief/desire analysis of my emotional state,[11] my anger would consist in, say, the belief that someone had intentionally harmed me and the desire that I not be harmed. But is that equivalent to anger? It seems to be compatible with my being frustrated instead, or simply sad, or just plain curious about why the person acted as she did, or only wanting her to stop it. For this to be *anger* must I not *also* conceptualize her as having done something *wrong*, for example, having harmed me *unjustly*? Is it possible to be angry and yet feel that no moral transgression has transpired? I begin to doubt that indignation, a distinctively moral emotion, is only a subcategory of anger and to suspect it is the whole of anger.

Again I would like to highlight the methodology of my philosophy, for it jibes so well with its substantive content. I have put anger under the "negative" rubric, as something whose presence *counts against* morality; furthermore I have given it pride of place in my reasons for becoming an amoralist. Can I justify this "objectively"? I don't think so. I simply state the correlation (between anger and morality) and leave it to you, the reader, to assess. Obviously there are some people in the world who value anger positively, or at least as necessary to humanity's overall well-being, for example, as a motivator to great actions. So what can explain my treatment of it? Well, insofar as I am truly insightful of myself, the answer is painfully obvious to me: Anger—my anger—has been a lifelong problem in my relations with other people. Therefore to realize that anger and moralism have an affinity has been an enlightenment. First, it could go a long way to explain why I have been such a moralist all my life, both personally and then professionally. (And/or the direction of causation could go the other way.) Second, that a world without morality could be a world without anger is just about the most wonderful thing I can imagine—as attractive and motivating to me as the kingdom of heaven is to a theist.

So both the theist and I, the atheistic amoralist, are enthusiasts.[12] What differentiates us is that only my enthusiasm does not presume metaphysical fantasies. Yes, mine does project an ideal that may be unattainable, but it recognizes it as such and can still take satisfaction from moving in its direction. I should add, however, that I have not given up on argumentation about ethics. Thus, as regards whether anger is necessary to achieve morality's goals, I can point, for example, to the way a person could be highly motivated to rescue some skiers who had been caught in an avalanche, without having to be angry at anyone (indeed, *despite* her anger at the foolishness of the skiers for going out under dangerous conditions). Just so, I now believe, one could be desperately motivated to rescue Hitler's victims, without having to be angry at Hitler, who, after all, was just as much the product of the forces acting upon him as was the avalanche. Yet when I make an observation like that, I may feel the brunt of some moralist's anger about my lack of anger.

Morality is hypocritical. Morality aids and abets our ego's desire to have its own way by disguising even to ourselves what we are about. Do you suppose it is only a coincidence that the vast majority of the time that you deem something morally wrong, it is something you don't like on other grounds? Do you suppose that your real motive when you are insisting on "the right thing" is love of morality? While I do not doubt that there is such a thing as *philomoralia* (having myself been a devotee these many years), I surmise that it is rare among the basic motivators of actions we deem moral. What makes us demand *justice* for ourselves, I would contend, is commonly our *envy* of someone who has more of something we desire than we have, or our *desire for revenge* against a person who has hurt us; and the justice we demand be imposed upon the person who has hurt someone else is often only a convenient and socially sanctioned channel for pent-up frustrations with our own life or an outlet for latent bigotry, prejudice, or envy.

A sure sign of the hypocrisy that is endemic to morality is "standing on principle." That the principle on which one stands is favorable to one's own interests or preferences is blatantly revealed by one's being content to "sit down," as it were, when that selfsame principle applies to others'. Thus, "all men are created equal," proclaimed the Founding Fathers, but of course, judging by the legal system they subsequently established, they held many men (including *wo*-men) to be "less equal" than others.[13] Do keep in mind, by the way, that I am not saying that racist and sexist egalitarians are morally *in the wrong* (since I hold *there is no such thing* as being morally in the wrong)—only that their moralism (insofar as they are moralist about their views, which they typically are) lends itself to being hypocritical. And hypocrisy (along with racism and sexism) is something I don't like, both in itself and because of its effects.

Morality is arrogant. Ego likes to primp and plump itself. This is called egotism, as opposed to egoism or selfishness.[14] Egoism and selfishness have to do with one's well-being, real or imagined, whereas egotism is a distinct trait that could even be at conscious cross-purposes to one's own welfare. For example, you might willingly sacrifice your health and even your life in order to achieve a personal sense of (not to mention, public acclaim for) your wonderfulness. Morality—that is, what I have called empirical morality, which involves believing and acting on a moral basis—is positively dripping with egotism. As one's moralism heightens, so does one's self-regard. There is nothing so soothing to egotistic craving as to take a firm stand against some perceived evil; and the greater the evil, the more flattering to oneself to oppose it.

Might Amorality Be Preferable? 43

This sort of posturing can reach orgiastic proportions. One typical place to observe this is at a murder trial—again, the more heinous, the better. Demands for the death penalty are often as bloodthirsty as anything one could imagine the murderer doing. Death may not be enough to slake the appetite for "justice"; the letters to the editor fantasize a painful and protracted death for the perpetrator "to match the crime."[15] That is, of course, further evidence of the *anger* and *hypocrisy* of morality, since what goes by the name of justice or retribution in these cases may be the thirst for revenge pure and simple. But it is also a grand opportunity for the egotism or arrogance of morality to strut its stuff, since the more despicable the evildoer, the more innocent and good and *"raised-above"* is the moral judge by implied comparison.[16]

The obvious objection to my way of picturing the above is that it puts cart before horse: We *are* morally superior to the malefactor, and hence entitled to scorn him, precisely because of what he has done and we have not. Well, this is another of those issues which seem impossible to resolve (in lieu of some ideal social science) without begging the question. I reiterate my methodological modesty: *See for yourself*, now that I have drawn your attention to the phenomenon, whether moralist invocations are saturated with egotism. But also recall that the argument of this chapter presumes the conclusion of Chapter 2, which is that morality does not exist. So of course we could not *in fact be* morally superior to anyone else, simply because, *ex hypothesi*, there is no such thing as morality. But there are certainly additional considerations; for example, the infamous Stanley Milgram experiments at Yale University are relevant to assessing our supposed superiority to a convicted murderer, since they suggest that most of us are capable of murder under certain circumstances.[17] So we might add self-delusion (or at least self-ignorance) to the list of empirical morality's unattractive qualities, since "there but for the grace of God. . . ."

However, I can also easily imagine my reader directing a *tu quoque* ("you also") at me, since am I not myself taking personal satisfaction in my superiority to the benighted mass of humanity that is so self-deluded about its moral superiority? Well, I suppose I am; and this could indeed be some atavistic moral pride on my part, for I do not expect ever to rid myself entirely of moralist attitudes, given than I identified with them for almost 60 years. Indeed, would it not be the *height* of arrogance for me to believe that little old *moi* was capable of completely overcoming what all flesh has been heir to? But I do not *mean* to be making any *moral* judgment about moral posturing (hence, not even my own!), or for that matter about taking revenge (which I might myself seek in some circumstances), or anything else. I am simply trying to describe the reality of what is going on so that both you and I can respond however we will to facts rather than fantasies. And my response to the factual (or perceived) linkage between egotism and morality is to allow my *definite dislike* of the former to attach to the latter as well.[18] For me, to feel the brunt of or even just witness the admonishments of one of morality's soldiers, not to mention suffering from their concrete actions, is like hearing fingernails drawn across a blackboard.

The move to resist, then, is this: from "I like Mozart's music more than any other" to "Mozart composed the finest music there is," from "Spitting disgusts me" to "Spitting is disgusting," from "This pleases me" to "This is good," from "I (or even 'we') don't like that" to "That's wrong." Who the hell do "I" think I am—God? Well, yes; "I" *the moralist* do indeed think and act like God (or Zeus), who looks down upon the world and the people in it and, based on His satisfaction or dissatisfaction with them, judges the former good or bad and the latter righteous or impious, their actions right or wrong. This turns subjective feeling into objective fact. If there were a God, maybe He could pull that off; after all, if He could create everything out of His own Will, then why not also the values of everything out of His own Taste? But when we mere mortals do it, the transmutation from psychological preference to moral reality is a delusion effected by sheer arrogance.[19]

Morality is arbitrary. Certain dialectical and rhetorical moves typify morality, chief among them supposed showstoppers like "Because it's wrong!" and "Because it's the right thing to do!" But, for all the rhetorical power they have, such assertions are ether empty of content or thoroughly ambiguous. Indeed, that probably accounts for much of their power: They can elicit assent because they are misunderstood or simply silence an opponent who has no clear idea of what they mean.[20] Were one to do without such verbiage, as amorality recommends, one would have to speak intelligibly. Needless to say this could put a lot of people at a disadvantage, for their reasons could then turn out to have far less appeal to their auditors once their actual import were understood.

Morality is imprudent. It may seem odd to categorize morality's imprudence as a mark against it. Is this not what distinguishes morality in the best sense, namely, that it asks us to make sacrifices on behalf of "doing the right thing"? But what I see now, as an amoralist, is mainly *foolishness* whenever someone insists on doing the right thing in the face of obviously bad consequences. And the reason I see it thus, I think, is that morality is *particularly* prone to imprudence or, for that matter, harm to anyone, whether oneself, another, or society. Why so? Because morality implicitly and explicitly claims to trump all other considerations. If morality were just another consideration to throw into the mix when deciding on a course of action, it might not appear quite so absurd to heed its voice to some degree, even when it counted against welfare. But given its defining nature as "the highest *telos*," morality can only be seen as a privileged bully or the gorilla in the room. Thus, it is reckless as well as egotistic.

I speak from vast experience, having been an arch-moralist for much of my life. How often I have stood on principle, like a veritable Washington crossing the Delaware but leaving a wake of tears shed by myself and others. Now from my amoralist perspective I marvel at my penchant for making myself and others miserable,[21] and all in the service of a mythical ideal. Thus, even when I had every (other) reason not to do x, if morality dictated that I must do x, I was very likely to do x. There were so many moral heroes swimming in my head who would have done the same, and so in a sense were guiding my behavior, even from beyond the grave, as conscience (or prior heroes) had guided their own. But now I see myself as if I had been hypnotized and commanded to squawk like a chicken without really having the faintest idea why, other than the command itself.

A trivial example that nevertheless captures the essence of this phenomenon: If you receive unsatisfactory service from a waiter, *justice* demands leaving a small tip, if any. However, not only will this displease the waiter, but it also increases the likelihood of even poorer service should you end up eating again in the same establishment and having the same waiter. For it is human nature that resentment and retaliation rather than self-chastisement and reform will more likely result from a hurtful act, however "justified." The way I reason now is: An *especially generous* tip will catch the waiter's attention and make him more likely to be scrupulous in future. Granted, this is only an empirical speculation on my part. But the point is that I now have a different objective: Rather than seeing it as my paramount duty to be a moral enforcer, I am only concerned to satisfy my desires (for good service and happy waiters).

Morality is intransigent. Morality lends itself to intransigence because it clothes our desires in absolute standards of what is good and right. Our wants thereby gain in stature and importance (in our minds) and may potentially reach unlimited extremes.[22] Thus, for example, a worker could quite naturally not only desire to earn enough money at her job to be able to provide better for herself and her family, but also believe that she has (by the good fortune of having been born and raised to be a person whose desires are in synch with Ultimate Moral Truth) a *moral right* to that level of wage. From this perspective, any opposite-tending interests of her employer are *simply irrelevant*. Negotiation is not even an option, morally speaking. The worker is right, so the employer must be wrong. She is good, so he must be bad. One does not compromise with evil.[23] Similarly, morality fuels the endless strife between members of a family or partners in a long-term relationship, who often have a simple dislike of each other's habits, but raise that to a higher key by branding them morally wrong or bad. Amorality, by contrast, is more ready to compromise and negotiate since it encourages one to see one's desires—*however intense*—as, just that: desires.[24] So the correct picture of the situation is of opposing desires, not good versus evil. True, as a rule nobody wants their desires to be frustrated; but even more strongly do we dislike being or being considered to be morally in the wrong. Recognizing that only the former is in question seems to me more likely, therefore, to lead in the run of cases to a mutually desirable[25] outcome.

Morality is useless. It is simply not informative to tell somebody (including oneself) to "do the right thing" because, as noted previously, that phrase is empty of content. It is true that I did spend the first chapter spelling out a fairly specific meaning for it; but a reality of the world is that different people mean different things by "morally right" and other moral phrases, and even one and the same person does at different times. In many cases, therefore, empirical morality is simply not performing the function of ethics, which is to provide a "guide to life" by telling us what to do. This makes morality often *worse* than useless, since a person you are advising or admonishing to do the right thing could have a meaning in mind that is quite at variance with yours. You simply cannot assume that they are going to receive the same counsel from their conscience that you would have received from yours. Much better then, I advise, to say what you mean. Thus, "Don't lie to her" or "If I were in your shoes, I would tell the truth," etc. Again, even in your own case, thinking that you ought to do the morally right thing may not advance your thinking one iota, for you may still haven't a clue as to what the right thing to do is.[26] And even if you did, it could be morally outrageous in the eyes of another; for example, "Steer an airplane into the World Trade Center." Morality's infinite adaptability, due to the indeterminacy of its content, can license anything, and at one time or another just about everything has been held to be the right thing to do according to somebody or other's conscience.[27]

Another way to think about why morality is peculiarly *unhelpful* is that, like much religion, it replaces effective intention and action with magic. In the beginning is desire: We want the world to be a certain way. Insofar as the world is *not* that way, we have two basic choices: accept it as is or try to change it.[28] If we opt for the latter, we have two choices again: do what is rationally required to change it, or invoke some Higher Power to do it for us. If we go the latter route, we have two choices again: Pray or propitiate God or the gods, or invoke a godless equivalent. I claim that morality is that last choice. We see that the world is not the way we want it, so we proclaim that it *ought to be* that way. But either this won't get us very far, and could even *inhibit* progress because of the opportunity costs, or else, as noted in the preceding paragraph, the fictitious endorsement of our desire could indeed strengthen its efficacy, but, similarly, our opponents will summon their own gods or morality to strengthen their desires, leaving all of us no better off and perhaps worse off. Morality therefore not only is frequently useless but often has downright disutility.

Morality is silly. Morality creates not only unnecessary practical problems but also unnecessary theoretical problems. In fact I have reached the point in my counter-conversion to amorality that I view the whole of normative ethics as on a par with theology. As Pope Benedict XVI humorously related in an address at the University of Regensburg on September 12, 2006, "it was once reported that a colleague had said there was something odd about our university: it had two faculties devoted to something that did not exist: God." Just so, normative ethics is a discipline that debates the relative merits of competing conceptions of a vast middle earth of morality. It might as well be trying to determine the number of angels that can dance on the head of a pin.

Thus, prior to my amoral turn, I was endlessly puzzled by the seeming relativity of morality. For example, it was crystal clear to me that I had every right to prohibit my stepson from playing his loud music in the house when it disturbed me; and yet I could not for the life of me see how my being put out by his loud music was somehow morally privileged over his being put out by my prohibiting him from playing it. Oh, certainly I could concoct any number of "principles" that would favor my "position" over his; but I felt in my heart of hearts that what it all boiled down to was desire and power. I was mistaking the strength of my desire for quiet for the truth of a principle of morality. And another: My ex-wife used to leave things on the kitchen counter, whereas I would put things away after I had used them. My thinking was that I should always leave the counter ready for someone else to use; but her thinking was that you need to give some slack when living with other people. I could never figure out a way to "prove" that I was in the right; all I knew was what I preferred. Now I believe that this is all there ever was and will be.

But then to see these homely instances transferred to the professional sphere was truly a revelation. I remember the moment it happened. I was attending a colloquium being given by an academic philosopher, who was defending a novel theory of why abortion is (sometimes) morally permissible. As a knee-jerk "liberal" I have always supported abortion rights. However on this particular occasion I was suddenly struck by the intricacy of the philosopher's argument and the absurdity of believing (or assuming) that some reasoning of this sort must underlie what, "in fact," makes abortion sometimes permissible. The abortion controversy in my country is going to be settled by non-philosophers on the basis of their gut feelings and preferences and the ensuing struggle for social and political power.[29] In a word, it's called democracy. To the degree that arguments are relevant, they will be ones that resonate with the general public and not ones that only a trained analytic philosopher could (just barely) understand . . . *not to mention* that the philosophers themselves will *never* achieve *anything close* to unanimity. I therefore raised my hand and asked my colleague, "Do you really believe there is a moral truth of the matter about abortion?" To my newfound amazement, she answered, "Yes."[30] Which is exactly how I would have replied but a few years previously.[31] Now I can only marvel at this attitude—just as I marvel at how "grown" people in 21st Century America can believe in religious miracles, even highly intelligent and educated people in Ivy League seminaries.

In addition to judging everything as right or wrong or permissible, there is among the moral the concomitant tendency forever to be seeking out new obligations in every nook and cranny of our lives. This is the bread and butter of some professional ethicists, especially the "applied" ones. Silly!

WHAT I LIKE ABOUT AMORALITY

Thus a partial inventory of what I do not like about morality. Now to things I like about amorality. It might be supposed that this would simply consist of the opposites of the above. But that is not how reality works. For example, just because morality tends to be egotistic does not prove that amorality would not also be; maybe egotism is an essential feature of the human soul, which will attach to *anything* we favor. But, yes, I would like to think that amorality has opposite tendencies from what I don't like about morality. I will discuss below what I have found to be the most salient likeable features of amorality in my own experience.

Amorality is guilt-free. The feeling of moral guilt—I am not talking about *being* morally guilty, since that has gone the way of the dodos along with metaphysical morality—is a ubiquitous pain in the human psyche and society. If we meditate or introspect we may be amazed, and appalled, by its prevalence in our motives and in our sense of ill-being. For me the discovery came in contemplation of Christianity: What it's all about is guilt! I should be no stranger to the phenomenon, as I am a nice Jewish boy for whom this feeling has always been more than a merely stereotypical trait. But it was still an eye-opener, or a way to gain perspective, when I had occasion in recent times to observe Christian liturgical practices firsthand. What the congregation seemed to be intent upon was relief from the burden of sin. While to all appearances they were perfectly respectable, plain, and loving people, their religious preoccupation bespoke a terrible inner turmoil about their own essential unworthiness. For they required nothing less than the supreme sacrifice of His only Son by God Himself in order to expiate our human sins, since they were so great and numerous as to be utterly beyond merely human power to do so.

I must admit to a rolling-of-the-eyes bemusement with this public ritual of self-flagellation in the guise of Jesus' Passion.[32] But I also took a dim view of it, and the entire institution built upon its foundation, since it struck me as a colossal diversion from more useful activities and investments of time and money. Would it not be far more helpful to the world to focus one's energy and resources on, say, Oxfam, rather than on supporting a local establishment for the recognition and removal of guilt, which devotes five percent of its budget to running a soup kitchen on the side? My cynical view of the church is that it is a perpetual guilt machine, which generates guilt for the purpose of motivating its further generation.[33] And ("secular") morality is surely in league with it, and perhaps in historical fact may be nothing but its bastard offspring, denying its own paternity.[34]

I too crave relief from the feeling of guilt, as I suggested above. Guilt follows me like my shadow. It second-guesses my every act and thought and feeling, no matter how trivial or momentous, or how admirable in appearance. Take my writing of this book: Couldn't I be doing something more directly beneficial to the world? Is it not sheer laziness and self-indulgence that explains my preference for a life of philosophizing, even if that activity partakes of the noble Pursuit of Truth and promises A Better World to boot? Well, I would like that inner voice to shut up. So in this I am exactly like the Christian at Sunday service. It's just that I think I have now come up with a way that is both more veridical and more effective for accomplishing this, namely, defending amorality! After all, if there were no such thing as morality (not to mention, sin) or, more to the point, no *belief* in morality, then the perpetual guilt machine would be effectively shut down; amorality would have sabotaged it.

Amorality is tolerant. In the United States one is free to practice whatever religion one pleases, or no religion, subject to various constraints that enable us to live together and enjoy equal civil rights and so forth. Part of the means of bringing this about has been a constitutionally enshrined prohibition on established religion. No doubt this grates on some who take their religion seriously, but for the most part Americans have seen the mutual benefit they derive from this policy. Possibly this is due to the history of religious persecution so many suffered that led them to come to this land in the first place; possibly also to the great variety of sects, which would make it difficult for any one religion to gain democratic primacy. But I suspect that another factor has been a societal sublimation of antidisestablishmentarianism into morality. For in this country one finds examples everywhere of laws or attempted legislation to enforce certain conceptions of right and wrong, whether about drug use, sexual behavior, or how to die. I have been involved in movements of resistance to the imposition of uniform standards in some of these areas, but previously I saw myself as a member of the moral opposition to religious subversion of the secular polity. Now I would say that the enemy has all along been as much morality as religion, for what I dispute is the quintessentially moralist conviction that one's preferences are intuitions of a universalizing imperative reality.

What a breath of fresh air is amorality's thoroughgoing tolerance. I can report "empirically" the wave of good feeling that washed over me as I became liberated from the obligation to oppose my neighbors at every turn (for, in my eyes, they had all been wicked to the bone). My current conception is that we all have different desires, but there is no question at all of its being my *duty* to try to stamp out some of them (whether mine or my neighbors'). I may, and do indeed have some desires that *conflict* with some of my neighbors', and so I remain motivated to try to change some of theirs and/or some of mine, or otherwise seek accommodation. The particulars will depend on the relative strengths of my own desires, for example, to further a certain "cause," to have my way, to get along. Strategy will loom large in my amoralist reasoning about what to do and how to live (ethics). But none of that will be imposed on me by anything other than my own net-desire. I need not also take account of, not to mention have it all trumped by, some external, absolute imperative.[35]

So instead of the squint-eyed and off-putting look of disapproval directed at my neighbor and his ways, I can greet him with wide-open eyes of appreciation. What a pleasure to be able to interact with others on a genuine, human basis, rather than as their robed judge. Even so, there could be any degree of disagreement between us. Thus, if somebody, thinking that amoralist tolerance goes too far, had asked me, "But what about bin Laden?" my reply would have been, "Stop him!" His continued freedom and even existence interfered with far too many of my strong desires for me to want anything other than his departure from the scene. But, as President Obama said after bin Laden was killed, "We don't need to spike the football." A respectful burial at sea was a suitable end to the public story; and again, not for moral reasons, but because, all facts and desires considered, this seemed both truer to the reality of bin Laden's essence as, like everybody else, the product of his culture, upbringing, experiences, etc., rather than evil incarnate,[36] and also the best way to achieve the United States' objective (or "collective desire") of minimizing danger for its citizens by not needlessly incensing others.

I prefer the tolerance of amorality in two ways, then: it's better than *being the brunt* of intolerance by officious busybodies, who wish to impose their values on me and others or, failing that, show their disapproval of mine and others';[37] and it's better than *carrying the burden* of intolerance toward others, whom I must judge and try to correct. The challenge that remains is for me to curb my intolerance of those who are intolerant. I do not want to say that they are in the wrong, morally speaking, but that they have false metaphysical beliefs,[38] which result in their having attitudes and doing things that I wish they didn't. Therefore I am motivated to employ various strategies that might be effective in turning them around, specifically, as with this book, to convince them of the falsity of their beliefs *and* of the preferability, to themselves, of a world of radical tolerance.

Amorality is interesting. When I see some of my religious friends waxing in praise of the Lord and His magnificent Creation I feel that I can empathize in purely secular fashion. All of my life I have been an amateur astronomer; and I could not be living at a better time, for this is the golden age of astronomy. The knowledge we are acquiring about the cosmos is beyond anything that could have been imagined. But that knowledge is also partially of new "mysteries," such as the recent discovery that the bulk of the universe consists of dark matter and dark energy, so-called because their nature remains opaque to us. When I mentioned this to a theist I know, she immediately enthused about this further proof of God's greatness. The very mysteriousness of it was for her the key; it suggested that only God could understand what was going on. But for me the mystery was exciting in the exactly opposite way: I saw it as a new challenge for science, which, I do not doubt, will be up to it.[39] Furthermore, its unraveling will reveal yet more wonders.[40]

In analogous fashion, I am learning to appreciate how interesting the world can be when moral conviction is replaced by boundless curiosity. Here is an example of a commonplace that became for me a source of fascination. I was driving down the street when, up ahead, I saw two teenage girls step off the curb. They were talking to each other and did not slacken their pace one iota. They gave no indication that they even noticed my car moving to intersect their path. I was going slowly enough that I did not have to slam on the brakes, but I did have to come to a complete stop in order not to run them down. They completed their crossing directly in front of me without so much as a by-your-leave. What struck me (about not striking them) was the novel attitude I had towards the girls when this episode occurred. In the "old days" I would have been seething with indignation. "What kind of idiots are you?" I would have thought-projected at them, perhaps via my facial expression. "You are *moral* idiots, because you know full well that I can and will stop; so your feigned indifference to my car coming down the road is really an expression of colossal selfishness, of complete lack of caring about my purposes in wanting to continue on my way and about putting me out, by making me brake. This is the essence of immorality (as Kant tells us); you are treating me as a mere means to your own end of crossing the street without *your* having to pause."

But instead of that kind of reaction, this time I was mainly *curious*. "What on Earth can they be thinking? How could two people reach their age and not give a thought to an oncoming car or its driver? What has their upbringing been like? What attitudes are they exposed to among their peers? Where did *those* attitudes come from?" *Et cetera et cetera et cetera.* Their behavior is a captivating problem, is it not? And my response to it was like Newton's suddenly realizing that being bopped on the head by an apple falling from a tree presents *a problem*. But perhaps that was only due to my ignorance, because I had not walked in those girls' shoes. For them it was as *natural* to behave as they did as for me it was *puzzling*. But, then, does not my puzzlement have *its own* history of a thousand sources? So that too could become an impetus to questioning; for example, *why* would I typically have been so *angry* at jaywalkers—a reaction that seemed *natural* to *me*? (Another apple bonks the noggin.) Even though I am thoroughly acquainted with myself, I have, like anybody else, only superficial knowledge of the springs of my own psychology. The questions can have intrinsic interest for someone to whom they spontaneously occur, but they obviously also have the potential to be of practical use.[41] For both reasons I am pleased by amorality's penchant for generating them.

Amorality is explanatory. Amorality has the potential to resolve various anomalies that beset morality. Consider the problem of so-called moral luck.[42] It seems to be a reality of our moral experience that we judge certain acts differently based on their outcomes, even if the intention behind them, or some other morally relevant factor, were the same. For example, a drunken driver who has accidently run down a child will be judged more severely than a drunken driver who ended up in a ditch, not to mention one who made it home without event. But "theoretically" this seems bizarre. Were not the drivers equally guilty or wrong for getting behind the wheel of a car in the first place? Why should the mere contingency of a child along the way in the one case but not the other make any moral difference? Yet even the law would treat them differently, imposing a far stiffer penalty on the driver who hit the child.

From the amoral or desirist point of view, however, there is little mystery. It is natural for desire to focus more on what has actually happened than on motives or other causal factors. Survival depends as much on avoiding the rockslide due to spring thaw as the spear hurled by an enemy. Intention and other factors do also have relevance to survival in various circumstances or for more tenuous reasons, such as maintaining group cohesion; but the primary object of our desires remains the immediate effect of an action. So while we would be more keen to subdue a person who ran down a child intentionally than a person who did so out of sheer recklessness, our desire to subdue the latter would be stronger than our desire to subdue a person who was only weaving down the road, even though they were equally reckless.

Amorality is simple. We have emptied the cages of the metaphysical menagerie of morality. Let us review the roster of mythical beasts who have escaped (or, more correctly, from whom we amoralists have escaped).

> Moral obligation and moral responsibility
> Moral rightness, wrongness, and permissibility
> Moral considerability
> Moral merit or worth ("desert")
> Moral goodness
> Moral rights
> Objective values
> Free will and moral agents
> Moral justification
> Conscience or moral sense
> Moral guilt

Incredible once you think about it, isn't it? And in their place . . . ? Well, in a way, nothing. Just as nothing was required to take Santa's (and the flying reindeers' and the elves' and the chimneys') "place" when we ceased to believe in him, because our parents had been supplying the presents all along. But in another sense a replacement was required, for after all, it became incumbent on us to supply the presents for our own children now that we could no longer rely on Santa to do the job. Just so, most of the slack left by the departed morality would be taken up by the desires that had all along been doing the heavy lifting; for example, my decision to brake for jaywalkers has probably always been motivated much more by intrinsic aversions to hurting anyone and to being sent to prison than by some moral injunction.[43]

But we now also have a replacement criterion to guide our actions in general, to wit: Figure out what you really want, that is, the hierarchy of your desires all things considered,[44] and then figure out how to achieve or acquire it by means that are themselves consonant with that prioritized set of your considered desires. For example, suppose more than anything else you desired a nonviolent world and a personal life of leisure as ends; if you realized that you valued nonviolence more than leisure, then you would be prepared to commit some sacrifice of personal leisure in order to help bring about a less violent world; but you would still strive to avoid *violent* effort as the means to bringing about the desired world because, again, you value a nonviolent world above all else. Of course there could still be great complexity and perplexity in these "figurings"; but they would be *simpler* than moral reasoning, in that none of the items in the above inventory need be considered. The questions all become straightforward empirical ones; or in the words of Joe Friday,[45] "All we want are the facts."

A great underlying motive for amorality is therefore to call a spade a spade. Don't tell me what I ought or ought not to do or what is righteous or wicked or good or evil or morally justified or unjustified or your right or my obligation, etc. Just *lay out the relevant considerations*[46] ("the facts") so that my desires can sort themselves out in reflective response. For example: "If you don't brake for the jaywalkers, you will likely injure or kill them and also wind up in jail." Enough said: I will brake! In general terms: Once you have collected and meditated on the facts, then, as I like to put it, *there is nothing left but to feel.*

Amorality is compassionate. A delightful surprise on the path to amorality is the wellspring of compassion that arises from within oneself once the clutter of moral categories has been cleared away. I am speaking now in somewhat "mystical" language since I was introduced to this notion through instruction in yogic meditation. That was way before my amoral days, but the idea was presented in nonmoral terms and so I need not reject it now. Needless to say I would, however, give it an empirical spin, having to do with the simple utility for survival[47] of being compassionate. Whatever the precise genesis turns out to be, the fact of our compassionate

"Buddha nature" is clear. I know it when, for instance, moral judgment cast aside, my heart aches to see the silent video of the prematurely aged Osama bin Laden davening and stroking his beard in front of his little TV set in his shabby room in his last hideout in Abbottabad. I attribute his movements to an unquenchable restlessness from being under self-imposed house arrest for years, which, furthermore, he knows is forever. I pity him intensely because of what it must be like to have absolutely no room (physical or psychological) to maneuver should even one shadow of a doubt about his divine rightness and eternal reward ever creep into his mind. I can fully empathize with that even from the very different circumstances of my own life, because in essence we are all caught in the same trap. I can still see the perfect sense in doing away with this man as was done; but I do not rejoice in it.[48]

Amorality is true. As I noted in my preliminary remarks in this chapter, this inventory of morality's drawbacks and amorality's advantages is a personal one. To what degree it will resonate with you or with the general public, not to mention how it bodes for a life or a society that would be more to our liking than what we currently enjoy or what a continued moral trajectory would bring us to, is not something I venture to predict. Therefore in the end I revert to my fundamental claim that *there is no such thing as morality*. In other words, even if the elimination of the belief in metaphysical morality and of the rest of empirical morality were *not* likely to make us feel happier or more satisfied with our lives and society, and even if you in particular were *not* to become favorably inclined to amorality after meditating and reflecting on the list of features of morality and amorality I have highlighted, I would still appeal to your *love of truth* in a last-ditch effort to convince you to abandon morality not only "in theory" but also in your actual living.

I do believe that was the sort of motivation that inspired the writing of my previous manuscript, *Bad Faith*.[49] But could it have sustained me as an amoralist? Very possibly not. Indeed, my writing of *Bad Faith* was an act of desperation to find a viable, not to mention welcome, way to live amorally. Had I failed to do so, I might have succumbed to self-delusion or disregard (analogous to how we usually deal with the prospect of our own death) in order to preserve my basic functionality and sanity . . . or settled for moral fictionalism as a necessary *modus vivendi*.[50] It was a genuine and joyful discovery that amorality had a great deal to recommend it, and this has resulted in the present book.[51]

There is an additional argument to be made on behalf of truth, however, namely that truth also has instrumental value. Falsehood is a flimsy basis on which to found reliable behavior since, if found out to be falsehood, the behavior based on it becomes liable to foundering. I think of a lapsed Catholic I once knew, who, on becoming disabused of Christian

Might Amorality Be Preferable? 55

mythology, took up all manner of "sinful" behavior. This is the risk of linking ethics to theism or any other falsehood, such as I claim morality to be too: should the falsehood ever be realized to be false, the ethics may go by the board as well. After all, both religion and morality link how to behave with some supernatural reality. Hence, one could implicitly reason, absent the supernatural reality, no more ethics.[52] Now, it may seem odd for me to be adducing this as an argument for amorality, when it sounds like a main reason to oppose it. But my point is that the belief in morality is inherently unstable in this way, and therefore we had best topple it before it falls on top of us. In its place we can then build something more secure.[53]

5 Is Amorality Just Another Way of Being Moral?

I have defended a particular conception of morality (Chapter 1) and the thesis that morality of that sort does not exist (Chapter 2). I have argued that a world which assented to this and acted accordingly would not necessarily be worse off than our current world from a moral point of view (Chapter 3), and that such a world might even be preferable from the standpoint of our considered desires (Chapter 4). Granting all of these as premises, however, one might still decline to draw the conclusion I have, which is that an answer to the central question of ethics, "How shall one live?" is "*Without morals.*" Why might someone balk at that suggestion? Because the very notion of amorality I have put forward could count as morality on a different rendering.[1]

There are two ways this latter contention might be maintained. One is that, as a matter of empirical fact, "morality" has all along meant something closer to what I have been calling "amorality" than to what I have been calling "morality." The other way to counter my call for an amoral regime is to grant that I have been correct about morality's meaning heretofore, but then to argue that it would make more sense to *reform* the definition of "morality" along the lines of what I have been calling "amorality"[2] than to retain the old meaning and thence discard morality. As I have already indicated that I don't intend to enter the ranks of the experimental philosophers, I will continue to finesse the first issue; but the second suffices for our purposes. In other words, the question becomes: Were we to grant both the nonexistence of metaphysical morality and the viability and even desirability of a desirist ethics, might we still want to *call* the latter "morality" and retain as much as possible of the old *empirical* morality? An analogy would be to defend the existence of unicorns despite the nonexistence of *horselike creatures having a horn on their head*, in light of the plausible *reforming definition* of "unicorn" as *a mammal having a single horn on its head*. There would seem to be no insurmountable problem to labeling rhinoceroses as unicorns.

I can accept the gist of this objection to my project but still offer the following twofold reply. First, I think that any definition or analysis of morality that is not simply changing the subject would retain certain elements of the concept of morality I characterized in Chapter 1, which are, so to speak, essential to the notion. Therefore any "reinterpretation" which omitted any one of them would be too fundamental for the remnant still to be sensibly called "morality."[3] The key element being denied by the new definitions is the metaphysical authority of morality; but without this, I claim, it just ain't morality.[4] The analogy to "unicorn" would be to argue that the significance of its horselike feature in mythology and elsewhere is simply too central to the concept to eliminate it (or make it optional) in the cause of vindicating the existence of unicorns.

But second, even if there were a plausible conception of morality that escaped my existential attack on its having omitted an allegedly essential element, I would argue that the connotative echo of the missing element would cause so much mischief that we would still want to dispense with moral language.[5] This is because its retention would inevitably bring along the rest of the attitudes and feelings and behaviors that have always constituted empirical morality,[6] and which, by the argument of Chapter 4, are baneful on balance. Analogously for unicorns: We might decide that even though it made perfect linguistic sense to call certain non-horselike animals, such as rhinos, unicorns, it would lead to so much misunderstanding that better not to use the term "unicorn" when talking about them. If the category turned out to be an important one, we would still have the option to use a more cumbersome phrase, like "single-horned mammal," or else coin a neologism (as in my case, "desirism").

VARIETIES OF NON-METAPHYSICAL MORALITY

To make my case still more convincingly, I shall forthwith examine four main contenders for the title of morality—moral naturalism, moral constructivism, moral relativism, and moral fictionalism[7]—all of which resemble in certain key respects what I have been calling "amorality," but none of which, I shall argue, meets both of my above objections to retaining an institution of morality.

Moral Naturalism

Let us take it as a given that there is no such thing as metaphysical morality, no fiat laid down by God or the universe that determines how we ought to live. Still, we now recognize that human beings are creatures of evolution, who have some very clear "intuitions" about how to go about things because we have survived the test of, well, survival. Most evidently, we all possess the very strong desire to go on living, which seems an obvious enough drive to have if you are going to be successful at going on living when there are so many obstacles in the way of doing so. We also have healthy appetites for food and sex, which similarly serve to prolong our and/or their own existence, given the sorts of creatures we are. But are we not just as assuredly solicitous of the welfare of others,[8] and due to analogous causes? A caring instinct would seem well suited to enhance the survival prospects of a community whose members possess it, and hence its own as well. Why not, then, call that natural instinct "morality"? Thus moral naturalism: Human beings are by nature constituted to have moral desires.[9]

One problem with this simple picture is that it appears to presume a uniform desire or set of desires emanating from or constitutive of our shared human nature. But while there is certainly evidence for various kinds of commonality among human beings, is that commonality fine-grained enough to ground a meaningful morality? If it were, then why would philosophers never be able to decide among their competing Kantian, utilitarian, and virtue-theoretic intuitions? And why would, say, proponents of "pro-life" and "pro-choice" be forever at odds about the permissibility of abortion? The main answer one is likely to hear from a moralist is that his or her opponents are mistaken . . . if not downright evil. But a desirist amoralist would say that the far more plausible resolution of these issues is that they have no answers. Nobody is mistaken, nobody is evil (or virtuous). When all is said and done, there are only conflicting desires.

Suppose, however, that a convincing case could be made for widespread agreement among moral intuitions. Would moral naturalism then have a sound basis? I would still argue "No." My reason is that moral intuitions are commonly conceived as analogous to factual beliefs; and just as the whole world could believe that the earth is flat and yet be mistaken, so the whole world could believe that wife-beating is morally permissible and yet, by moralist lights, be mistaken. In other words, moral naturalism would seem to leave no room for moral reform. If the whole society enjoyed and approved the public spectacle of drawing and quartering a convict, then somebody with the sensibility of Montaigne would have no moral authority.[10] But surely, if anyone has moral authority, Montaigne does. Therefore to accept the problematic premise of moral naturalism that morality consists in precisely those moral desires that are widespread, is only to pluck the theory from the frying pan and plunk it in the fire. Granted, a desirist amorality fares no better. But amorality does not aspire to ground moral authority (because there is none), whereas it is the whole point and purpose of moral naturalism to do so.

Moral Constructivism

Time and again my espousal of a desirist amorality has been greeted by, "Oh, so you are a Humean"—the point being that I have not really forsaken morality but only traded in my erstwhile Kantian morality for a Humean one. The latter holds, roughly, that attributions of right and wrong (or virtuous and vicious, in Hume's character-based morality) are in fact psychological projections of "sentiment" or "passion" or, as I prefer, desire. This is opposed to there being some objective quality of the world external to our minds that makes things right or wrong.[11] Hume recognized, in addition, that moral sentiments vary from time to time and person to person and so on, whereas morality's judgments are presumed to be constant and uniform. He therefore introduced an artificial element by which morality is to be *constructed* from its natural components: We are to assume a "common point of view" for the purpose of assessing the objects of our moral judgments.[12] It would then be the deliverance of one's sentiments from *this* point of view that determined the moral rightness or virtue of whomever or whatever was being morally assessed.

But is this "common point of view" really unbiased itself? For example, to Hume it seemed eminently reasonable that the, or a, standard for judging the moral rightness or wrongness of things was a utilitarian one. For this reason did he famously reject "monkish virtues" as in fact vicious because useless.[13] But there are societies or communities—the "monks"!—that reject this criterion or at least give it less emphasis than Hume did. Therefore only Hume's own sense of what is moral could win this argument, but that would be question-begging, would it not? In other words, the common point of view seems not to be a divestment of biasing elements from one's actual point of view so much as the assumption of a point of view having certain theoretically-favored characteristics.

This is not necessarily something to be despised. My criticism is only that it would be presumptuous to suppose that the theoretical point of view one favors is any less subjective than the actual point of view one started with. For—my refrain in this chapter—what the moral ethicist, who in this case is a constructivist, seeks to establish is the *authority* of morality, namely, to prevail over any and all competing (types of) judgments and inclinations. But every attempt to devise or "construct" a point of view that is sufficiently God-like for this purpose, I maintain, will be doomed to construct or create a God in one's own image . . . even if, like Hume's, that "God" were anticlerical.

Now, the desirist amorality I advocate is also constructivist in that it advises "processing" our natural desires rather than simply taking them "raw" or "going with the flow." Furthermore, the recommended processing is of a sort that Hume would certainly have approved, namely, critical reflection on relevant information. But my brand of constructivism is not *moral*, and hence is unlike Hume's, because it does not aim to establish any kind of absolute authority for what it defends. The deliverances of our considered desires will be just that—desires considered. They will not be authoritative dictates or judgments or truths about value or how to behave.[14]

Moral Relativism

The two previous attempts to ground an empirical morality on something other than a metaphysical morality have failed. Both foundered on the shoals of moral diversity because the kind of moral authority they seek to justify presumes either a natural or a constructed unanimity of moral intuitions, but each of these is problematic for such reasons as have been given. Why not, then, take the bull by the horns and relativize morality? For example, let polygamy be wrong in Society A and obligatory in Society B, and that's the end of it.

Support for such a scheme comes from a functionalist conception of morality, which holds that the worthiness of a moral judgment or injunction comes not from some ultimate and intuitive categorical imperative but instead from the efficacy with which following a certain set of rules helps to preserve a thriving society or meet some other widely desired goal.[15] Since human beings live in a variety of geographical, historical, and cultural settings, it is only to be expected that morality will assume different forms from one place and time to another. Also, there can be alternative ways of filling the same function with comparable efficacy. Therefore morality is multiple, and no one morality is superior to all of the others.

As reasonable as that sounds in broad brush, however, a closer look at how the relativist scheme might work reveals problems. Suppose that the folks in Society A held that lying is wrong and the folks in Society B did not. Does this mean that the A-people believe that the B-people would be wrong to lie? Suppose they did believe that; then wouldn't they be mistaken? After all, according to moral relativism, right and wrong are relative (in this case, to a given society). Suppose then that the A-people believed it was morally permissible for the B-people to lie; then what the A-people really believe is that only they themselves should not lie. Would that make sense in moral terms?

It seems dubitable that the latter way of looking at things conforms to what people normally take morality to be like. If something is wrong (or right or permissible), then isn't it supposed to be wrong for *anyone* to do it?[16] I for one find it jarring whenever someone says something like, "Well, it would have been wrong *for us* to exterminate the Jews, but it wasn't wrong for Hitler." Yet this is indeed how an explicit relativist speaks. To me it is as bizarre as if someone were to hold that "It's true *for us* that the earth is round, but it wasn't true for the Babylonians." This strikes me as simply an imprecise way of saying that we *believe* the earth is round, but the Babylonians did not. And yes, we believe *that it is true* that the earth is round, but we also recognize that a belief can be *false*.[17] Moral relativism ignores the belief-like logic of morality by equating the belief that something, say lying, is wrong, with lying's *being* wrong. But I think most people understand that someone can believe that lying is wrong (in general or on some particular occasion) and yet lying not be wrong (in general or on that occasion).

I maintain that moral relativism is better understood as a sociological claim than as a meta-ethical truth.[18] Thus, according to some societies and/or individuals, female circumcision is wrong, and according to others it is permissible. But none of these societies or individuals would be relativist in their moral outlook; they would think of morality as absolute and

Is Amorality Just Another Way of Being Moral? 61

universal. Only the sociologist looking down from on high would be able to discern the sense in which their moralities were relative. But the members of the society that thought female circumcision was wrong—*including even the native sociologists*—would tend to believe that it was wrong also in the society whose members thought it was permissible.

It follows that moral relativism is not a *normative* thesis; that is, it does not ascribe *authority* to any explicitly relativist moral claim, such as that female circumcision is wrong. Moral authority only attaches to claims that are universal in scope, even according to moral relativism as a sociological thesis, which *does* still grant the universal scope of moral claims *as people in fact intend them*. Thus, the claim that female circumcision is wrong is intended by the members of Society A as applying to themselves and also to the members of Society B, just as the members of Society B believe that female circumcision is permissible for themselves and the members of Society A. This explains why everyone *believes* that moral claims are authoritative, but at the same time it removes the *legitimacy* of that authority.

I myself am a moral relativist in this way. And far from contradicting my amoralism, I think it is one of the best arguments for it. For when I try to imagine a sociologist who is a moral relativist in the same way but who also is herself a moralist, I see only incoherence. And this is a real phenomenon. It may even be the norm. For without an explicit embrace of amorality, which is rare, the average social scientist remains a muddled moralist in light of his or her sophisticated analysis of empirical morality. This is because they have no recourse to any "tie breaker" among competing moral systems that is not tendentious or question-begging.[19]

I will give one more example to clarify what I am arguing since this is so important for the amoralist project. In my own experience it is common to come across a person—typically a politically liberal academic (like myself)—who is completely conversant with the utter contingency of moral beliefs, which correlate so well with one's upbringing, socioeconomic status, political leanings, and so forth. Nevertheless this person will continue to subscribe to the moral beliefs that correlate with his or her own political leanings, etc.; and when I say "subscribe to," I mean with the same gut commitment and tenacity as the most naïve moralist.

But why do I think this a problem? After all, could not the same be said about our factual beliefs? In the United States, for example, it seems pretty clear that one's belief or disbelief in biological evolution is likely to correlate with one's upbringing, etc. Yet not for one moment does my understanding of that sociological fact weaken my own commitment to the truth of evolution. "Nor should it," I am also tempted to say. However, recall from Chapter 2 that there is a difference between the moral situation and the factual situation. According to the "best explanation" of the world, there is indeed a tie breaker between true and false factual beliefs, but when it comes to moral beliefs, their relativity is better accounted for by their *universal falsity*.[20]

Now, an ethicist of the relativist persuasion could still hold out for the stronger claim that everyone *should* conceive morality as inherently, and not just factually, relative. In other words, all of us who assume that there is a single moral truth or single set of moral truths (which happily conforms to our own moral beliefs) should wake up to the fact that this is not so, and instead recognize that morality is essentially functional and hence liable to variation from one cultural setting to another. This would be a reform movement, and it would indeed bear a great similarity to desirist amorality, which sees a diversity of desires or outlooks as fundamental to ethics. It would also restore to relativist moral pronouncements a certain authority, which rested not in their universality but in their functionality.

However, I would then revert to my other objection to retaining empirical morality—and specifically, moral language—despite relinquishing metaphysical morality, which is that moral language would still connote the universal authority of morality that its new denotation denied, and hence genuine reform of empirical morality would be hampered by continual confusion and conflation. This is why I advocate starting with a clean slate—eliminate moral language so that the attitudes and behaviors that it naturally elicits will be suppressed, and those that it suppresses be elicited—and I advise instead calling a spade a spade. State explicitly what you mean—that is, to put the point in the hypothetical manner I am advancing, do this if you wish to avoid the (in my view) baneful effects of retaining moral language and enjoy the (in my view) beneficial effects of relinquishing it that I described in Chapter 4.

Moral Fictionalism

The most straightforward way to preserve a morality that lacks metaphysical underpinning, namely as relativist, simply does not work. This has led to a final theoretical act of desperation: Retain full-blown absolutist, universal morality, but *as a fiction*.[21] Why do this? Because empirical morality does have its good points[22]—not even the amoralist denies that but only argues on the basis of a preponderance of bad—and in any case may be a habit we just can't break completely. So let us embrace the fiction of metaphysical morality with a fiction of our own, namely, that morality is a fact. But we will have defused the really noxious stuff by withholding our sincere endorsement of the airy nothing, for in our heart of hearts and mind of minds we will know we are only playacting.

My hunch, however, is that this delicate dance of pretense will be taking place in a mine field, with explosions of genuine moralism always but a step away. As I myself have become more adept at speaking and thinking amorally, I have become more comfortable with empirical amorality as a practicable alternative to empirical morality; and so I simply see no need to hold onto the moral paraphernalia. Even more to the point: The longer we indulge in moral pretense, the longer we put off being able to reap the full benefits of amorality.[23] After all, moral pretense is not simply a continuance of empirical morality, but requires acquiring a new mental expertise: balancing empirical morality with a fundamental disbelief in its basic premise. So the empirical question before us is not whether it would be harder to develop a new skill (of empirical amorality) than to maintain the status quo (of empirical morality) at which we are already adept, but rather whether it would be harder to develop one new skill (of empirical amorality) than to develop a different *new* skill (of moral pretense). And since the latter would seem to be far subtler and hence more difficult to perfect and more prone to lapses[24] than would be the straightforward abandonment of moral thinking and speaking, I'd wager that the latter would be more effective in achieving their (presumed) common goal of maximally satisfying our considered desires.

Thus, all four attempts to "save" morality as an empirical institution bereft of metaphysical underpinning have failed, each for its own reason. Moral naturalism assumes an implausible unanimity of moral intuitions; moral constructivism employs a question-begging method of achieving unanimity; moral relativism gives up on unanimity but thereby lapses into incoherence; and moral fictionalism, in a last-ditch effort, reappropriates the discredited metaphysical foundation of morality in a collective pretense that is, I have argued, unwieldy if not unworkable. But even supposing that any of these objections could be met, all of the theories suffer from at least one of two additional major shortcomings. There is first and foremost the failure to account for the normative force of morality. A theory may "save the phenomena" of moral language, behavior, and feelings more or less, but still not explain why anyone is *obligated* (*tout court*) to act or to live accordingly. Thus, anybody with a clear-sighted understanding of its literal substance would be moved to say, "But that's not what I *mean* by morality." The other problem is that putting any of these theories into practice would still expose us to the ills of empirical morality, while denying us the benefits of amorality that were characterized in Chapter 4. In sum, therefore, the proffered substitutes for amorality lack the original authority of the moral language they continue to employ while retaining its troublesome trappings—the worst of both worlds.

ATTACKING A STRAW PERSON

Before closing my case against morality, I am compelled to revisit an assumption with which I began this chapter. My argument has placed a great deal of emphasis on the "connotative baggage" of morality, whose contents I spelled out in Chapter 4. But it is not implausible for someone to object that I have been conflating morality with moralizing. Thus, it is easy enough to find instances of people wielding morality like a brick, but, the objection goes, that only shows they are putting morality to improper use or don't even know what it is. We certainty recognize the

64   *Ethics without Morals*

difference between a genuinely moral person and someone who has got it all wrong.

In fact, this is a general phenomenon: People are proficient at turning things into their very opposites, whether intentionally or unwittingly. Perhaps the most obvious analogy to the moral case is reasoning: One can use logic and argument in the pursuit of truth, which is *reasoning proper*, or to prop up one's own position regardless of its merits, which we refer to as *rationalizing* precisely to distinguish it from the real deal.[25] So the objection is that my argument for amorality has been tendentious because I have only given examples of *moralizing* in order to discredit *morality*, but these are quite different things, and I have been attacking a straw person.

Well, of course I grant that moralizing is not the same as being moral. However, the objection has less force than it appears to. Recall first of all that I have been arguing for two distinct theses, namely (1) There is no such thing as (metaphysical) morality and (2) Reflecting on that and other considerations would move us to prefer giving up empirical morality (the belief in metaphysical morality and the feelings and behaviors attendant thereon) as well. The objection applies only to (2), the desirability of giving up empirical morality, since the objection does not address the argument I gave in Chapter 2 for (1), the non-existence of metaphysical morality. The issue before us, therefore, is whether, knowing or believing that morality does not exist, we would prefer to live the Noble Lie that it does exist.[26]

I think not, for the reasons given in Chapter 4. And the reason the argument of Chapter 4 escapes the charge of conflating morality with moralizing, let me now argue, is that the charge commits a conflation of its own, namely, of empirical morality with conceptual morality. We tend to appraise morality based on its concept. I myself am drawn to the concept of morality as I have characterized it—as the Kantian injunction to respect persons; and I have also explained how I strive to retain its essence in an amoral fashion, that is, as an ideal rather than as an obligation. But I have been concerned to appraise *empirical* morality on a different basis, namely (and as befits its label), an empirical one.

In other words, what attitudes and practices does the belief in morality tend *actually to bring forth* in human beings? So, for example, if we subscribed to Kantianism not as a subjective value or ideal but as something we and everybody else *must*—in the sense of absolute obligation—implement, would the resulting world be preferable (that is, as always, more to "*our*" liking)? Of course my answer—for myself, and my hunch about others—has been "No." My critic's argument, therefore, mistakes the concept of morality for the reality of morality, that is, for what a hard-eyed look would reveal about the effects of trying to live up to the concept and otherwise applying it in the world.

One final remark: Although I have conceded for the sake of argument that there is such a thing as moral behavior and attitudes that are not moralistic, I am not, in truth, certain of that. There may be something about the human appropriation of morality that makes it irredeemably objectionable to our considered desires.[27] At the least I would expect my critic to provide some convincing examples of unadulterated, that is, non-moralistic morality.[28] It is not sufficient for the critic only to *label my* examples as "moralistic" and thereby dismiss them as not what he is talking about. I sense that there is a great deal of special pleading going on, and the pleas begin to pile up like the epicycles in Ptolemy's theory of the universe. Another image or metaphor that comes to mind is peeling an onion: Once we have removed all the cases of moralizing, will there really be any examples left of a pristine morality? I sometimes suspect that the label "moral," as opposed to "moralistic," is being applied as a mere honorific, specifically, to those instances of moralist behavior that my moralist critic happens to approve.[29]

THROWING THE BABY OUT WITH THE BATH WATER

Still there is the nagging doubt that we could not do without morality. Even granting that empirical morality does have many undesirable features, including those we label "moralizing," would not giving it up nevertheless amount to throwing the baby out with the bath water? Again consider the analogy of reasoning: Are we prepared to turn our backs on it just because it is so often misused? Why not view the bad stuff as an occupational hazard of pursuing a good "occupation," in the present case, of being moral? Thus, we accept the hard bargains that every police force has its rogue cops, fire departments attract arsonists, many lawyers are shysters, and many doctors are quacks. There can also be undesirable biases that are unavoidable in necessary institutions, such as the tendency of doctors to view their patients as more or less ill, psychiatrists to view their clients as more or less crazy, etc. As the saying goes, "To a hammer everything is a nail." Just so, the commitment to morality no doubt engenders erring on the side of moralizing, with all the ill effects that entails. But can we afford to give up morality any more than we could afford to give up medicine and law and policing and firefighting?

Yes, I reply, sometimes there is a baby in that bath water . . . but sometimes not. Sometimes it's just an old sock that is too filthy and too flimsy to be worth wasting any more time trying to clean so that you can keep wearing it. I think empirical morality is like that sock. Reasoning is something I certainly desire to retain, despite its own penchant for misuse; but voodoo, astrology, superstition, religion, etc., I could do without altogether. The question is: Which model better fits morality? Again, I don't know the answer although I have my opinion and have given my grounds for it; so all I am concerned to do in answering these objections is resist the suggestion that something other than the epistemic uncertainty that is endemic to the human condition stands in the way of our giving up empirical morality.

To many moralists, empirical morality is just another tool in our arsenal for defending the society we desire, or even the very possibility of society. To give it up would be like being obliged to fight with one hand tied behind your back. But suppose that were true. The problem with releasing the second hand is that *everybody* has that second hand, including the people you believe are evil; they see *you* as evil. Therefore empirical morality breeds escalation of conflict, which is often to no one's net benefit.[30]

Thus, the cure is sometimes worse than the disease. My current favorite example of the truth of that maxim is the War on Drugs. This quite-literal war is minimally effective in reducing drug usage but meanwhile gives rise to humongous problems. I cannot imagine a surer means of maintaining drug cartels, military dictatorships, political corruption, street crime, the spread of disease and addiction, etc., than to keep drug usage and manufacture illegal rather than regulated.[31] Just so, upholding empirical morality in order to control undesirable behavior in society may be counterproductive, or at least be likely to bring more ills in tow than would the amoral alternative—like going after a fly with a shotgun instead of a swatter.

So the aim of dumping out all that bath water while holding onto the baby would be defeated. The tub is not likely to be drained; and the real problem is the baby—or, as I prefer to think of it, the old sock.[32]

6 How Shall We Treat Other Animals?
A Case Study in Applied Amorality

If ever there was proof of the bankruptcy of morality, it is its application to nonhuman animals.[1] That sounds like a moral condemnation in itself, doesn't it? And originally it was for me. My personal inclination was to detest the abusers of animals. What they do is the epitome of the unconscionable because other animals are the epitome of innocence and vulnerability. But the problem does not stop there, not by a long shot. Human beings have gained absolute power over all other creatures on this planet, and with that has come a nearly total abandonment of restraint in our dealings with them. Perhaps the most notorious example of this is factory farming, wherein so-called food animals are treated as mere unfeeling objects having no basic rights even to freedom from pain and early death.[2] Furthermore, their numbers are literally astronomical: We kill as many animals to eat *per year* as there are stars in the Milky Way Galaxy—on the order of 100 billion.[3] And the vast majority of this unprecedented (and ever increasing) slaughter is not only unnecessary for human nutritional and even gustatory needs, but downright counterproductive of human and ecological health.[4]

Meanwhile, the sorts of "moral justifications" that are given for these practices are laughable. We are told that animals do not experience conscious pain,[5] that they have no interest in their own continued existence,[6] that they lack immortal souls.[7] I will not waste my time or yours refuting such nonsense. It is obvious that these "arguments" are purely tendentious and self-interested.[8] Even so it could reasonably be asked in what sense have I been making a case against *morality* if I have only been refuting (or, to be frank, simply dismissing) the moral arguments *in favor of* factory farming and, more broadly, meat eating and using animals in general? Must I not also reject any and all moral arguments *against* the use of animals?

I think that observation is correct. And to begin with let me point out that it is not only animal abusers who marshal the kinds of arguments I trotted out on their behalf but also some animal advocates. This is because many, in fact probably most people who care about animals still believe there is a difference between use and abuse. For example, isn't there a world of difference between a cow in a factory farm and a cow on a family farm? And don't we all love our pets and treat them like members of the family?

68   *Ethics without Morals*

Therefore animal advocates who believe that the answers are obviously "Yes" to such questions conclude that our concern should be for the welfare of animals and their humane treatment. They see this as the golden mean between, at the one extreme, simply exploiting animals and, at the other extreme, having nothing to do with them.[9]

But the counterargument is that, while indeed there is a conceptual difference between use and abuse, its playing out in real-world terms is problematic at best, tenuous or elusive at middling, and a pretext for exploitation at worst. In the final analysis there is no difference between the human use of animals and the abuse of animals, or, as we may also put it paradoxically, between their human use and their inhumane use.[10] The most obvious way to think about this is to consider that all of the individual instances of use are dependent on *institutions* of abuse.[11] For example, even the beloved and pampered pets of the typical American household represent untold violations of animal integrity and well-being in the breeding, housing, transportation, and frequent abandonment of such animals.[12]

MORAL ARGUMENTS TO ABOLISH THE USE OF ANIMALS

But that refutation only delays the reckoning for an amoralist such as myself who still wants to advocate for animals. For what, then, of the moral arguments in favor of *abolishing* the human use of other animals? Am I not implicitly endorsing *these*? Here again, however, I answer "No" since I no longer believe that any of them work.[13] Let us take a look at the strongest moral defenses of this *abolitionism*.[14] One is based on animal welfare and the other on animal rights.

The Welfare Argument

The first is the more common. This argument recapitulates my remarks immediately above about the equivalence of use and abuse. There is such an extreme power imbalance between human and nonhuman animals in the modern and especially in the contemporary world that the human exploitation of animals is inevitable. Therefore so long as we countenance any institutions of animal use at all we will be aiding and abetting the suffering and premature deaths of countless animals. But *it is wrong* to aid and abet such suffering and death because of the moral (in this case, utilitarian) imperative to maximize happiness and/or minimize unhappiness in the world. Therefore we should end all use of other animals and just let them alone to live on their own terms.[15]

While I certainly concur with its central premise, the argument ultimately fails because its conclusion simply does not follow. This is because power imbalance is a constant of human relationships that we approve or at least tolerate as unavoidable, including with other humans. Think of parents and children. Think of teachers and students. Think of people with and without disabilities or retardation. Think of middle-aged adults and elderly adults. Think of police and civilians. Think of judges and juries and defendants. Think of prison guards and prison inmates. Think of doctors and patients. Think of natives and immigrants. And on and on. Does it follow from this that all relations among these groups and all the supporting institutions should be abolished, and all human beings live in isolation, each to fend for him- or herself? Of course not. Indeed, the very thinkers who highlight such imbalances tend to advocate a heightened interaction, not a reduced one. For example, while feminists note the pervasive oppression of women by more powerful men, they also note our fundamental interdependency in all things. This is why the feminist ethics tends to be one of caring.[16] Although the sort of feminism that advocates for the complete separation of the sexes can certainly be found, it is not the mainstream. Men and women may be from Mars and Venus, but we all now live on Earth. Not too many people are advancing the proposition that we "go back where we came from."

Why, then, would the power imbalance between humans and animals be an argument for their wholesale separation? Indeed, does not the environmental movement, echoing feminism, build upon the ecological insight that there is interdependency throughout nature?[17] Furthermore, the argument for abolition fails to take into account all of the human benefits that derive from our use of other animals. These must be part of the calculation if our concern really is to maximize welfare in the world. Finally, the argument ignores the glaring fact that without the human use of animals, most of those animals would not exist at all, since they are only bred for human use and most would be unable to fend for themselves without human care. So at the very least some additional premise is required to demonstrate that welfare maximization for sentient beings on this planet could be achieved only by the universal segregation of humans from other animals. For example, the utilitarian abolitionist might argue that it would be better for domestic animals if they did not exist at all than that they exist under the conditions they do, or, more tellingly, *could*, even with further reform. But this would be a notoriously difficult proposition to prove.[18]

The Rights Argument

One response to the above rebuttal of the welfarist argument for abolition is to revert to a welfarist *position* on animals.[19] By the latter I mean the view, introduced earlier in this chapter, that animal use can be distinguished not only in theory but also in practice from animal abuse, and so the concern of animal advocacy should be not the abolition of animal use but rather its reform, in other words, the assurance of humane treatment focused on animal welfare.[20] This is where the second main argument for abolition comes in, which is based on animal rights and not animal welfare. The central idea is that all animals, human and nonhuman, have inherent value and worth, and hence merit due respect. Our animal worth is attributed to a certain quality we possess in common. Typically this quality is deemed to be autonomy,[21] which is the capacity to decide or determine our own destiny within the limits of our natural and social habitat.[22] The second premise of the argument is that due respect of this sort means recognizing that all animals are entitled to exercise their autonomy, and the third premise is that humanity's use of other animals always involves violating that basic freedom we owe them. *Ergo*: It is always morally wrong for human beings to use other animals, regardless of welfare considerations.

The reason the argument concludes this only for other animals even though the argument is based on a feature that humans share with other animals is that human beings alone have the capacity to *consent* to being used by (fellow) humans.[23] Consent is an act of freedom or autonomy (that is, when sufficiently informed, etc.), so it is not a violation of someone's autonomy to use them if they have explicitly or implicitly consented to it, other things equal. For example, there is nothing morally wrong about using a teacher to gain instruction, or using a car mechanic to have your car repaired, or using a doctor to have your illness cured, etc. That is, in the normal run of cases. If you cheat on your exams, or fail to pay your repair bill, or lie to the doctor in order to get a prescription, then it could plausibly be argued that you have abused them because you neither sought nor obtained their consent, nor is it plausible to presume it in these cases, and hence you have done something morally wrong. But animals do not have the power to say, "OK, you can eat me" or "OK, you can experiment on me" or even "OK, you can keep me locked up in your apartment all day except when you take me outside on a leash." They may not have this power only because they do not speak our language, or we do not understand theirs. So alternatively we could say that, even granting that other animals do have such a capacity—and there are certainly pet owners and ethologists who would vouch for that[24]—it is fairly obvious that they would not or *do not* consent to most of the uses we humans make of them.[25]

Now, note in particular that autonomy is not a guarantor of welfare or happiness. This is why the rights defense of animals is fundamentally different from the welfare defense. It *is* possible to imagine a welfarist autonomy defense, according to which the best way to provide for the welfare of other animals would be to let them run their own lives in a natural habitat, since, presumably, they are well suited to do so by the grace of evolution. But this runs up against the common problem of all utilitarian arguments, as we also saw above in the attempted welfarist defense of abolition, which is that the truth (or falsity) of such an assertion is impossible to ascertain.[26] One could adduce relevant considerations ad infinitum and never resolve the question. For example, don't pets live far longer and less stressfully than their wild counterparts? Yes, but they are denied the pleasures of freedom to go when and where they will, of exercising their inborn talents to hunt or forage, of raising their own families, etc. But a rights defense does an end run around all that and says, "Consequences be damned, we must respect the autonomy of all sentient beings." One consequence (or implication) of *this* is that the rights program if implemented could lead to a world in which animals were *worse off* than they are now. This does not faze the true rights theorist.[27] Autonomy simply trumps welfare in the rights scheme of things. These are competing intuitions, and all of us are capable of responding to both. But if one of them has the advantage in a moral defense, as the rights view now appears to do because of its ability to bypass the insoluble problem of determining which of multiple possible states of affairs would be the optimal one, it will be preferred by the moralist.

As persuasive as the rights argument has been to many, however, I myself no longer believe it is sound. The reason is the one that has motivated this book: There is no such thing as morality or objective value. This implies that there is no such thing as the inherent value that all animals, including ourselves, are supposed to have and that supposedly accounts for our having moral rights. You may love your kitty for her own sake and wish only her welfare and happiness and provide her with them as best you can; but this has nothing to do with the metaphysical assertion that your kitty *deserves* your good wishes and beneficence or, *a fortiori*, that you *owe* them to her. Furthermore, while neither you nor I doubt for a moment that your kitty possesses the autonomy to decide her own movements and preferences, it simply does not follow that your kitty has any *right* to exercise her autonomy or have us respect it—not even any *prima facie* right, other than, that is, whatever *legal* rights our society may be inclined to accord her as an expression of *our* autonomy.

WHAT IS AN AMORALIST TO DO?

Thus in brief my reasons for becoming disaffected with the morality of animal ethics. Qua moralist I am firmly in the abolitionist camp. But none of the moralist arguments are sound because, in the final analysis, morality itself is a phantasm. Therefore . . . what? Have I given up on abolitionism? Am I now indifferent to the suffering and slaughter of other animals? Hell no. But then on what basis do I maintain my commitment to the cause? My first reply is: Isn't that a silly question? I am reminded of the Buddha's parable of the wounded man:

> It is as if a man had been wounded by an arrow thickly smeared with poison, and his friends and kinsmen were to get a surgeon to heal him, and he were to say, I will not have this arrow pulled out until I know by what man I was wounded, whether he is of the warrior caste, or a brahmin, or of the agricultural, or the lowest caste. Or if he were to say, I will not have this arrow pulled out until I know of what name of family the man is;-or whether he is tall, or short, or of middle height;

or whether he is black, or dark, or yellowish; or whether he comes from such and such a village, or town, or city; or until I know whether the bow with which I was wounded was a chapa or a kodanda, or until I know whether the bow string was of swallow-wort, or bamboo fiber, or sinew, or hemp, or of milk-sap tree, or until I know whether the shaft was from a wild or cultivated plant; or whether it was feathered from a vulture's wing or a heron's or a hawk's, or a peacock's, or whether it was wrapped round with the sinew of an ox, or of a buffalo, or of a ruru-deer, or of a monkey; or until I know whether it was an ordinary arrow, or a razor-arrow, or an iron arrow, or a calf-tooth arrow. Before knowing all this, the man would die.[28]

The Buddha likened the wounded man's questions about the provenance of his wound to metaphysical questions about the soul, the afterlife, and so on, which he saw as not tending toward a solution to the more pressing problem at hand. In the Buddha's case, that problem was the suffering of mankind. In my case, the problem is the human tyranny imposed on other animals. For both of us the point is to solve the problem. So even aside from the unsoundness of the arguments for abolition, my complaint is that the whole argumentative pursuit is useless or worse than useless. It is *perhaps* useful to study the moral arguments of the *opponents* of abolition, the better to be able to refute them. But to counter with moral arguments of one's own *in support of* abolition is both futile and bad strategy: futile because no sound argument exists, and bad strategy because one will therefore be put at the same dialectic disadvantage as one's opponent of having to defend the indefensible. This is also why I used the qualification of "perhaps" in the sentence above, since even to engage opponents solely for the purpose of *refuting* them risks involving one in a fatal turnabout. Moral dialogue is a tar baby.

So suppose I, the amoralist, refrained from moral arguing and debating with people who do what I do not like, which in the present case is: use other animals. What, then, would I *do*? A range of options suggests itself, among which are the following:

> Be scrupulous in my personal avoidance of animal use, but otherwise adopt a passive stance of live and let live (which in the case of other animals means, "let die," i.e., be killed and abused by people who feel differently from me).

> Be scrupulous in my personal avoidance of animal use, and use rhetoric or deceptive and fallacious arguments and tactics to bring other people around to the same position.

> Be scrupulous in my personal avoidance of animal use, and take up arms against the people who do use and oppress animals.

Since I am an amoralist, I see any of the above as fair game; that is, none of them would be *morally wrong* (nor, of course, morally right or even morally permissible). However, even I have grounds (so to speak) for opposing all of them: *I don't like them.* It is essential to realize that an amoralist—like anybody else—has desires regarding not only ends but also means. Sometimes a person has a kind of desire that encompasses both.[29] In my own case, I have two of these, that is, desires that exert a global influence on all of my other desires. They are (1) a certain image of myself and (2) a certain ideal of the world. The self-image that I desire to embody is of a person who is, among other things, compassionate, activist, and honest. The world-ideal I desire to promote is of a world in which all people have those same qualities. The two global desires could therefore collapse into the second one, with myself as a single instance; but I keep them separate because I could be striving to mold myself even if I felt stymied by the world, or for that matter, I could continue to try to change the world even if I found my own nature to be incorrigible.

My global desires then apply to the three options listed above as follows:

> To be passive regarding other persons' use of nonhuman animals would evidence an insincerity on my own part, which is incompatible with my cherished image of myself as one who really cares about the suffering of others. Of course the caring itself provides a direct incentive for being active on behalf of the other animals.

> To employ rhetoric and other tactics that are intentionally fallacious, misleading, etc. would violate my cherished self-image as a person of integrity. I also happen to feel that I am poorly equipped to engage in those tactics (if only for lack of practice!) and, more generally, that they comprise a less than optimally effective strategy (although I could be mistaken about that).

> To employ or encourage violence, sabotage, intimidation, and other such tactics to further the cause of animal protection and liberation is something I am simply "constitutionally" averse to (no doubt due primarily to upbringing and circumstances; for example, I went to a Quaker school for 12 years). I also take a dim view of such tactics as incompatible with my world-ideal of straightforward and respectful dealings among all people.

EXTREMES OF MORALIST RESPONSE

Before discussing further options, I want to contrast my amoral responses to the three options above with some moral responses. I see two extremes of possible moral reaction that, in my view, count against morality. One has to do with one's purely personal behavior, which in all of the cases above was to refrain from using animals oneself to the greatest degree that is reasonable.[30] The other has to do with one's behavior towards other human beings who continue to use animals, which in the above ran from minding one's own business to coercing or even killing other people.

Weakness of Will

What I find telling in the case of personal behavior is that morality can be utterly toothless. This was brought home to me by the news that two moral philosophers (that is, philosophical ethicists who believe in morality) with whom I am acquainted both agree that it is wrong to eat animals, but they both continue to do so, pleading "weakness of will." Weakness of will is a notion beloved of moral psychologists (that is, philosophical psychologists who study moralist attitudes and behavior) who enjoy puzzling over things, in this case, how somebody could believe something was wrong and yet still do it. But it also serves the very practical function of giving moralists a supremely easy "out" from practical responsibility, as this example shows.[31]

Meanwhile I myself, who do not believe in right or wrong any longer, have been so moved by what I have learned about the plight of "food animals," since taking up animal ethics several years ago, that I have been a dietary vegan for the past three years.[32] I seek no praise for my sacrifice; nor do I wish to condemn those who eat animal products. I view my change as simply cause and effect: I cannot help but be a vegan, given what I know and who I am. But from the standpoint of a *moralist* who believes that eating animals is *wrong*, which of the following is the better state of affairs (and who the better person): (1) that a person is convinced that eating animals is wrong but still eats them because of weakness of will, or (2) that a person does not believe in right or wrong, but does not eat animals because he cares more about their welfare or liberty than pampering his own taste buds?[33]

Violence

At the other extreme from the ease of moral evasion, but equally telling, I feel, are the lengths to which morality can push a person to act. Thus, when I contemplate the range of options for dealing with other people who use animals, from letting them alone to follow their own moral compass, to forcing them to follow mine ("or die!"), I see an inexorability in morality's moving toward the latter. It seems to me quite plausible that a moralist who reflected on the animal question with sustained seriousness would come eventually to endorse the more extreme forms of animal activism. For it is a potent combination of facts and feelings to contemplate the enormity of what human beings do to other animals. Survey the whole from, as it were, the microscopic to the telescopic: from the tiny mouse, whose sentience, emotions, and personality are readily knowable to anyone who takes the time to look, to the aforementioned astronomical figure of abuse—hundreds of billions of innocent creatures of every kind subjected to a life of confinement or other cruelty before being summarily slaughtered. To take such things to heart is enough to make an Old Testament prophet out of anyone. And if God will not rain down punishment on the perpetrators of this abomination, then it is up to the individual activist to try to stop it . . . *by any means necessary.*

Speaking from my own experience as a former moralist, I would say the only way to keep a level head is to bury one's head in the sand. If one believes in right and wrong and good and bad, then nothing imaginable could be more evil than animal agriculture, animal experimentation, hunting and trapping, the pet industry, kidnapping (or breeding) wild animals for zoos, circuses, and aquaria, and so on. To rationalize these practices morally would be an act of philosophical desperation. To face them unblinkingly, if one has a human heart, is to be moved to cry: "Never again!" So if you know that in a building across town, male chicks by the thousands are being thrown alive and fully conscious into a meat grinder[34] . . . what are you going to do? It is the same, I imagine, for a person who opposes abortion as the slaughter of the innocent because she really believes that an embryo is a conscious person. I don't believe that, but I can empathize with the person who does and therefore feels justified to do *whatever is necessary* to abort the next abortion. There is no question, however, that the nonhuman animals who are used for food and research and so forth are fully conscious beings of their kind. So how could one know this and *feel* this and then sit idly by?

Of course there are more ways of taking action than "rising up," and nonviolent action may well be more effective as well. My point is only that, for a moralist, the question of violent action against animal users is a real one. Unless one's moral philosophy counseled total pacifism, such that you would not approve even sending in the SEALs to "capture or kill" bin Laden, or a SWAT team to rescue your child from an armed madman, it is hard to see how you could be morally opposed *in principle* to using violence against people who were actively engaged in acts of cruelty to and killing of animals, not to mention on the massive scale one finds today. Most Americans would already want to see severe punishment meted out to the person who tortured or killed their pet or kidnapped him to be sold to a pharmaceutical laboratory. Why would it not be the moralist's job to open pet owners' eyes to the comparable wrongdoing in which the pet owners themselves are complicit if they are not vegans (and, indeed, if their pets came from a pet store or a breeder rather than a shelter), and then draw them to the further conclusion that, besides reform of personal habits, extreme measures might be justified to bring that wrongdoing to a quick and total halt? This would seem especially the case in a society that is *not* set up to send in the SWAT team to rescue chicks and pigs and cows from the slaughterhouse or rats and cats and monkeys from the research lab; so

76 *Ethics without Morals*

it is left up to the citizens themselves. In the end one can only ask: Which is the more violent society—the one in which animal activists do whatever is necessary to bring a quick and total halt to the unnecessary slaughter of hundreds of billions of sentient beings, or the one in which that slaughter proceeds undisturbed?[35]

But I don't believe any moral argument for violence is sound. That is mainly because I don't believe there is such a thing as morality. If I did believe in morality, I think I would be hard put to answer some animal activists' arguments in favor of violence.[36] Most likely there would be the typical situation in moral debate, which is that a stalemate arises between the proponents of the opposing views, who would each have scored points against the other, but who would remain unpersuaded by the other because each also has hold of, or has been gripped by, some strong intuition; and so they will leave the dialectical forum and return to their practical business, moved as they are by their respective desires.

But as an amoralist I can tell you quite simply why I want no part of violent tactics or strategy: The requisite attitude that supports it would make my life in society untenable. Indeed I speak from experience. When in a moralist frame of mind, I do get so worked up about the *evil* of animal use that I cannot have any kind of normal intercourse with humanity at large, nor with just about any individual, no matter how close to me, since the vast majority are willing accomplices to atrocities. I begin to feel like "a stranger in a strange land." I literally have images forming in my head of what it must have been like to be a person of normal conscience (i.e., the kind you and I have) who was living in Nazi Germany, even amongst one's own family and friends.

And this is precisely what makes animal ethics the perfect "test case" for morality. For animal use is so widespread, and so accepted, that a person who thinks otherwise and, indeed, with a clear moral vision sees it for the evil it is (morally speaking and by my moral lights), will naturally harbor a universal hatred for its perpetrators, i.e., human beings.[37] In a situation such as this, one would have to be God-like or saintlike to sustain an attitude of tolerance and forgiveness on the ground that "they know not what they do." Most of us, and certainly myself, are neither God nor saint. So our morality would likely take a severe form if we stripped away the appearance of innocuousness from people's daily habits of eating and the biomedical establishment's routine practices of research and on and on to gaze on the ugly reality beneath.[38]

Once again I need to remind my reader that I am speaking only personally. I can readily imagine the rebuttal that even in Nazi Germany there were individuals who courageously if resignedly accepted what I myself am shying away from, namely, total *emotional* isolation from one's family and friends and society because of antagonism to the prevailing attitudes and practices, if only in secret (the better to be effective). Were these not moral heroes? My reply is twofold. First: Yes, surely there is such a thing as a moral hero. Just as there were no doubt also *Nazi* moral heroes in abundance, for example, people who killed the "non-Aryan" "human vermin" despite their natural compunction and even revulsion for the task (since the "vermin" often looked very similar to non-vermin, even to the Nazis' own families, but of course appearances can be deceiving) *because they thought it was the right thing to do.* So this proves nothing about the objectivity or reality of morality. Second, I see nothing in principle that requires allegiance to morality in order to withstand popular pressure to conform. For example, would not most of us spontaneously protect our own family from the Nazis, not because "it was the right thing to do," but simply because we love our family? I think the answer is obviously "Yes." And if so, why not suppose as well that most of us are capable of a comparable concern beyond the family?

So in being relieved from the isolating effects of moralism, I do not thereby automatically become a conformist. Far from it. I have actually become more isolated than ever, for now I not only oppose animal use but also oppose my former activists-in-arms who base their animal advocacy on morality! I am indeed a man without an ethical country, for even though there are a few fellow citizens of the Land of Amorality, there may not be any besides myself who live in the district of Animal Abolitionism. The saving grace, however, is that I am no longer distanced from all other people on the planet by *contempt* for them. Many of them may, and surely do find me peculiar, and some even hate me. But, as the expression goes, "that's their problem." As unpleasant as it certainly is to be hated (or dismissed, etc.) by others, the most corrosive kind of hatred is that which a person feels oneself toward others. I dare surmise as well that the former is often a function of the latter.

But a moralist animal advocate might still object that by ceasing to condemn animal users in my heart, I have become less effective in ending the use of animals.[39] To this I have two replies. First is, again, that I am speaking for myself. Thus, it could well be that I am the sort of personality who, although spontaneously provoking it, finds confrontation terribly uncomfortable. So that even if confrontation were more effective in promoting the causes I care about, I would care *more* about avoiding confrontations, not to mention seeing my society disintegrate into civil war. Perhaps my preference is the knee-jerk reaction of a privileged American "child of the '60s," who went to a Quaker school for his basic education, "dug" peace, love, and rock 'n' roll in college, idolized Gandhi, and certainly didn't want to go fight in Vietnam. Similarly, while I sincerely want all animals to be free(d), I *infer*—from observing my own feelings and actions—that I have the *even stronger* desire that human beings not be harmed or murdered. I cannot *"justify"* the relative strengths of my desires, but, as above, I can at best only *explain* them. Or perhaps I *could* give arguments in favor of my preferences, but the "buck" would have to stop somewhere, and that place would be at a desire or an "intuition." For example, no doubt one of my rock-bottom commitments is to humanity as such, so that in various situations, although by no means in all, I would favor a human being over another animal simply in virtue of the former's species. This is known as *speciesism* in the literature of animal ethics, and critics of animal use liken it to racism and sexism in the purely human sphere.[40] I can do nothing but acknowledge the truth of this attribution,[41] although I strongly suspect that there is not a single animal advocate who would not be speciesist under any circumstance.[42]

But secondly, I must remind the reader that what is now at issue is—to use the terminology I have introduced—the desirability of empirical morality rather than the truth of metaphysical morality. For since there is no such thing as (metaphysical) morality, the only question is whether we might still have good reason to continue the pretense or even delusion that there is. I have given my argument in the preceding chapters for a general answer of "No." In this chapter we are considering how this applies to animal ethics in particular. I believe that, for all we can tell at any rate, alternatives to violence would be more effective in achieving the long-range goals of animal abolitionism. I will certainly grant, however, that my purely personal disinclination to violence could be coloring my views about its objective (in)efficacy. But it *is* my view that the moral animosity of the animal movement—violence being only its most extreme outward (and to date mostly hypothetical) form—has backfired by shutting down the possibility of fully open dialogue among the parties to the dispute. This is a roadblock I encounter on a daily basis in my attempts to engage in *respectful* activism as an animal advocate.

It is true that "revolutionary" strategy sometimes takes that kind of result into account, seeing it as a benefit. The idea is that radicalization of the populace is furthered by pushing the powers that be to adopt repressive measures in a misguided effort of self-protection.[43] My own sense, however, is that, while that can no doubt occur in some situations, it is not likely in 21st Century America on this issue. There is too large and broad a constituency of meat eaters here to make any kind of widespread sympathy for such tactics likely. Far more likely is what, indeed, has already happened: The violent or even "merely" *intimidating* activities of a tiny minority of animal activists have handed the perfect pretext to animal users and government officials to smear the entire animal movement and even legally brand it as not only violent but *terrorist*.[44]

AMORAL TACTICS FOR ANIMAL LIBERATION

What then are the tactics or strategy that I favor? Here are some suggestions for furthering the animal-abolitionist agenda:

1. At the top of the list is to make sure that animal users and supporters of animal use are fully informed. And there are several key things to be informed about that are relevant to the case. These include:

1a. What nonhuman animals are really like. People in contemporary American society already seem to appreciate that dogs and cats have minds and emotions, feelings, intelligence, can be in pain or can be happy, and so forth. What they do not seem so receptive to is that this is also the case for the animals they eat and wear and the animals who are experimented on in medical laboratories, etc. Therefore I would strive to impress upon the human population that all mammals, including rats and mice, as well as all birds, including chickens and turkeys, and probably all fish[45] are fully conscious beings, even unto possessing individual personalities. There are of course many means of conveying this sort of information, including books,[46] television and film documentaries,[47] and firsthand acquaintance.

1b. How nonhuman animals are actually treated in our society. Until very recently the realities of factory farming and vivisection and circus life and fur hunting and trapping and so forth were kept as closely guarded as the formula for Coca Cola or, for that matter, the ingredients of soylent green.[48] Now it is possible to watch gruesome footage of all of these activities at the click of a "mouse."[49] Even so, most people seem to be unaware . . . if only because they refuse to look. That latter presents a special problem, but the first item to deal with is the simple ignorance that many people have about what is actually going on. I myself was entirely innocent of most of the horrors until a few short years ago, despite my being generally informed and specifically interested in animal welfare. So I now support the redoubling of efforts by animal activists to spread the word[50] (and also, of course, to acquire the information and evidence in the first place[51]). Here again there are books and media in abundance to help in this effort.[52]

1c. The costs of animal use to human beings and hence the benefits to human beings of ending that use.[53] Salient items in this regard are environmental depredations of all kinds, and health implications.[54] Most Americans are certainly unaware of the United Nations' indictment of animal agriculture as a leading cause, perhaps the leading cause of global warming.[55] (Of course global warming itself is a hard sell to Americans, but that's another albeit related story.) But that is only the tip of the (melting) iceberg.[56] Most significantly, perhaps, is that the domestication of animals for food has visited the major plagues on humanity.[57] It is also responsible for diseases that, in the popular mind, are pinned on vegetables.[58] Meanwhile the health advantages of a vegetarian diet seem well established.[59] The most recent health alert due to our carnivorous habits is the growing ineffectiveness of antibiotics for combating human disease due to their extensive use on farm animals to maintain their health under the crowded conditions of their husbandry.[60]

2. It is my belief, or faith if you will, that most people in our society would be moved by sufficient exposure to the above information to want to end the human use of other animals, at least to some degree or other.[61] However, they might still be stymied by insufficient knowledge of how to go about it or unavailability of needed resources. Once again the provision of information becomes key—this time about alternatives to animal use and how to cultivate or obtain them. I see a commitment to personal veganism as central.[62] But how does one become a vegan? It is not just a matter of not eating or otherwise using animals. Real practical knowledge and skill are required. Not to say that this is by any means daunting, only that it is something one needs to put one's mind to.[63] I know from my own experience that I wanted reassurance that I could give up eating all animals and animal products, such as eggs and dairy, and still receive my required nutrients without having to have a bland diet or devote my life to becoming a master chef or having to pay a fortune or move to a major metropolitan area. Over time, from both research and hanging out with vegan friends, I received this assurance, and as a result have been a happy vegan these three years going on forever.
3. Finally, it is my belief or faith that, having made the commitment to personal veganism, one will naturally seek to spread the Good News (so to speak!). A cynic could say that misery loves company, but I think it is equally obvious that so does concern, and also joy. Once again information becomes critical to the task. One now wants to know how to inform and persuade others to follow the same path as oneself. But there is nothing at all novel about this. One has available all the same sorts of resources as anyone else who wishes to teach others and change the world, from simple modeling of the transformation in one's own life to vigorous marketing and lobbying in the public sphere. There are as many ways to go about this as there are individual people in individual circumstances. For example, it must be obvious to my reader that I am doing this very thing by writing this chapter.

But my larger project in this chapter has been to illustrate with a single case study how amorality can hold its own in any project that would be pleasing to a moralist, and perhaps even do better than morality at achieving morality's own goals, or at least the all-things-considered goals of my reader, moralist or not. I have argued specifically that morality leaves much to be desired in the defense of nonhuman animals from human onslaught. For one thing, moral arguments are commonly enlisted in the defense of animal use by human beings—indeed, not only in its permissibility but even in its obligatoriness![64] But even the moral arguments *against* the use of animals are unsustainable. In their stead, I, in my capacity as an abolitionist regarding the use of either animals or morality, have offered a plan of action that is designed to appeal to the heart as well as the mind.[65] The heart of the heart is this: To the person who forthrightly (and amorally) declares, "I like my steak!" I would say, "Fine, but this only tells me that you care more about satisfying your taste buds with a familiar sensation than about the suffering and slaughter of harmless sentient beings. If this conforms to the image of yourself that you most value, and that you would like other people to retain of you, and, for that matter, that you would like your children to emulate, then I will talk to somebody else about how we treat other animals." Naturally I would hope that remark led the meat eater to reflect further on his dietary habits and eventually reform them.[66] But if it didn't, telling him that he was "bad" or did "wrong" certainly wouldn't do the trick.[67]

7 What Is Ethics?

In this book I have argued for two main theses: (metaphysical) morality does not exist, and (empirical) morality is best given up. A needling critique of my amoralist project persists, however, which is that I myself remain wholly true to my supposedly erstwhile moralist self in the pursuit of it.[1] For am I not implicitly *enjoining* the reader to give up moralizing? Have I not in effect concluded that it is *wrong* to moralize? Do I not, therefore, trip on my own feet as I reveal myself to be still very much a moralist? And is that not itself a kind of argument for the inescapability of morality—if the advocate of amorality should find it impossible not to moralize in the very act of pressing the case—as something which, however much we might wish to and be able to minimize its ("empirical") expression in our lives, nevertheless exists ("metaphysically")? There is simply no way around this, the moralist concludes: Just as it is hopeless to try to invalidate reasoning by reasoning that one ought to forswear reasoning,[2] or, like the skeptic, to insist that one knows that one can know nothing, so my arguing against morality refutes itself.

I believe, however, that I have broken out of this vicious (or perhaps I should call it "virtuous" since it argues for the *maintenance* of morality!) circle. Recall that in Chapter 4, I answered the charge of *tu quoque* by admitting that I might personally be faulty or self-contradictory in my emotional response to certain morally hued situations, simply because some habits are difficult or impossible to break, but I denied that that response was necessary to my critique. This image comes to my mind: One can know for a certainty that the stick one has inserted into the water is straight, but for all that it may continue to "look bent." Perhaps an even more apt, also aquatic analogy is peering over the side of a bridge into the rushing stream beneath and feeling oneself moving in the opposite direction from the flow; for I am often swept away by moral feelings even now. But this is only because, as one needs to do to experience the second illusion, one has narrowed or bracketed one's field of view to the stimulus, whether it be the flowing water of the stream or some human action or trait or person one is accustomed to cognize as wrong or bad or evil. Removing my cupped hands from my eyes, I recover my sense of standing on an immobile bridge.[3]

Similarly, without the blinkers of immediate emotion, I am able to perceive that *neither* a person severely slapping a child, *nor* another person moralistically berating the slapper, is doing anything morally wrong (*nor right nor* permissible). Instead they are both doing something that I very much don't like and want very strongly for them to stop doing; and so I would be motivated in both cases to intervene, albeit whether I would or in what manner would depend on the further circumstances (just as if I were a moralist). For example, it might be best to let the moralizer keep at it if this seemed to contribute to stopping the slapping, which would likely be my more pressing concern; alternatively, shutting up the moralizer could be the more effective way to stop the slapper if, say, the slapper were *acting out* some resentment at the moralizer. Meanwhile, yes, I think it is highly likely that I would, in addition, experience moral outrage regarding both the slapping and the moralizing; but I need not, and, I also believe, in the run of cases better if I did not, since my outrage, being based on nothing but habit, could well interfere with my execution of effective action in realizing my considered desire (of rescuing the child, in this case).[4]

Additionally, I would answer the suggestion that I am still a moralist by pointing to how that could be mistaking a description for an assessment. For example, when in Chapter 4 I complained that morality is hypocritical, it may have seemed that I was making a moral critique. But hypocrisy is a morally neutral concept; and I was only making two descriptive assertions, neither of which was a moral assertion, to wit: (1) The belief in morality frequently leads to the witting or unwitting imposture of immoral[5] behavior as moral (that's the hypocrisy), and (2) I don't like that (i.e., I dislike hypocrisy).

Here is another example, which is really exquisite. Person A objects to something Person B has done and cries foul: "That's not fair!" Clearly Person A does not like unfairness (whether directed at herself or anybody else). But Person B, it so happens, has a different "philosophy" and could not care less about fairness; he only wants to win, "by any means necessary." So now Person A plays the moral card: "But that's not *right.*" Enter myself: I don't like Person A's moralist move. Why not? Because it's unfair! She is trying to gain the upper hand by invoking an all-powerful mythology. So I am just like Person A in disliking unfairness, but quite unlike Person A in my unwillingness to be hypocritical or deceptive.[6]

The point is that fairness is not an inherently moral concept but simply a description of a certain kind of behavior. That is why this example shows both that desire (in this case, that there not be unfairness) is doing the heavy lifting in many supposedly moral episodes, and that empirical morality can be objected to on nonmoral grounds. In this case, the nonmoral objection is to giving the moralist an unfair advantage in disagreements about desire. This is something which I find intrinsically distasteful, that is, not because unfairness is immoral, but because "I just don't like" unfairness.[7]

But the moralist will likely still not be satisfied. Have I not got the whole point of morality wrong? Morality is about justification, not explanation. My argument to the best explanation in Chapter 2 was that all moral phenomena, such as believing in right and wrong and then feeling and acting accordingly, can be explained without recourse to metaphysical morality; so the latter drops out as superfluous. But the function of (metaphysical) morality, the moralist declares, is not to explain why we believe in it and so forth; clearly those things do have causal explanations like anything else in the natural world. But morality *justifies* those beliefs, feelings, and actions.

For we want to know not only *why*, say, somebody believes that lying is wrong, but also whether that belief is *true*. A causal explanation could answer the first question: She believes lying is wrong because she was taught that by her parents. But a different order of explanation is required to answer the second question of why her belief is *true*, and this we call a justification. The reason why her belief that it is wrong to lie may be *true* would be that *lying is wrong*, and *not* that her parents taught her that lying is wrong. The situation is exactly analogous to our believing that the earth is round. What makes that belief *true* is not that we learned it in school but that *the earth is round*.

As neat and tidy as that account is, however, I hold that it is not an account of ethical reality. The gist of amorality is that there is no such thing as moral justification. The very problem in search of an answer is not a real problem. The correct analogy is not the belief that the earth is round but the belief that the earth is flat. We understand why that is false: because the earth is not flat, but round. So the only real question is why some people believed that it was flat. This is explained by the appearance of the planet from the perspective of a relatively small and gravity-bound inhabitant of its surface. Just so: Since morality does not exist, the only issue regarding the belief that it does is why people have held that belief. The answer is likely along the lines of our having been taught that it does, and ultimately because it must serve some purpose in the evolutionary scheme of things, plausible candidates for which are not difficult to surmise.

I understand that my reply might seem to be question-begging in that it presumes the nonexistence of morality, when the existence of morality is what is ultimately at issue. But I am drawing attention to the question-begging nature of the requirement of moral justification, since *that* presumes that morality *does* exist. Meanwhile, I have given an argument (in Chapter 2) for why the latter assumption is less warranted than the former.

Look at it this way: There are two pictures of the world. In both there is empirical morality, but in only one of them is there also metaphysical morality. In the world that has both types of morality, a mystery presents itself: How do we ascertain that our beliefs about morality conform to the reality of morality? Have we some special sense organ for this purpose? Conscience comes to the rescue; it provides us with an intuitional gateway to moral reality, so we can know that a lie is wrong in the same direct way that we can know that an apple is red. But we have neither located any such organ nor conceived any mechanism of moral intuition that would be analogous to sensory perception; and so for this picture to be a correct portrayal of the world, we would need to postulate not only a transcendental moral realm but also a parallel metaphysics of ourselves, complete with ghostly intuition-organ, which somehow connected up with our physical brain and body to yield empirical morality. This would be a full-fledged Cartesian dualism of morality.

Contrast that to the other picture of the world, which contains only empirical morality. Here there is no mystery at all about how we could be in contact with a metaphysical realm, for no such realm is depicted. Once we have explained the phenomena we know, there is nothing left to be explained. And a naturalistic account of the world seems sufficient in principle to do the job. Therefore the burden of proof is on the moralist to justify the notion of moral justification, given that the assumption of morality seems only to create unnecessary, not to mention insoluble problems.

AN AMORAL ETHICS

I can still imagine a moralist reader scratching his or her head, or indeed even a reader who has been largely convinced by the argument of this book. Perhaps the remaining puzzlement is best put in this way: If there were no empirical morality, how could there even be ethics? For isn't ethics the inquiry into how to live? But if we are taking as given that there are no absolute values, and, in particular, no such things as moral obligation and moral justification, then how could ethics advise us? What sort of answers, not to mention supporting arguments, could be offered for questions like, "What *should* I do?" or "How *ought* a person to live?" Indeed, how could such questions even be asked? It would be like asking how long is the King of France's beard (since there is no king of France).

I do believe there is still a place for a robust ethics in an amoral regime. In fact, I believe ethics has been a fruitless enterprise exactly insofar as it has been conceived as an inquiry into morality. First let me review two reasons I have previously put forward for believing the latter. One is that morality has a very poor track record of resolving practical ethical questions. Has it resolved any at all? Chapter 6 made the case for the bankruptcy of morality in establishing how human beings ought to treat other animals. But, truth be told, morality can and has justified any and every act or attitude or style of life one would care to consider, including those that *other* moralists would deem heinous. Hence it has *resolved none*.

The second reason for understanding why an ethics focused on morality would be fruitless is that, even in those cases where morality points to a stunningly clear answer (in some particular moralist's eyes), it often does astonishingly little work in *motivating* someone to implement the answer. Chapter 6 gave the example of people who are convinced of the wrongness of eating meat, and yet who, with total clarity of mind about the compelling argument for not doing so, continue to eat meat. So on the one hand, moral inquiry gives you any answer you like; and on the other (but by the same token), if it gives you an answer you don't like, you can just ignore it. What, then, would be the point of this sort of ethical inquiry?

Still, I need to make good on my assurance that an *alternative* to morality exists that would turn *ethics* into a robust enterprise at last: one that would both "give answers" and motivate their enactment. A positive account of desirist amorality is therefore in order. In Chapter 4 I expressed this in the following maxim: Figure out what you really want, that is, the hierarchy of your desires all things considered, and then figure out how to achieve or acquire it by means that are themselves consonant with that prioritized set of your considered desires. This, it seems to me now, is the essence of ethics.

Note how it addresses the problems that have been raised about morality on the one hand and amorality on the other. First of all, the maxim is not any kind of categorical imperative, so it is not itself a moral injunction. It is purely advisory—take it or leave it. It seems to me to be a good idea, indeed, a great idea; but that's me and I cannot speak for you. I have done my best in this book to convince you of its sense and appeal; the rest is up to you. Second, it provides a definite procedure for answering practical questions. True, it will likely yield different answers for different people and even for the same person at different times; but that is the price to be paid for cleaving to reality rather than to a metaphysical dream. Finally, it guarantees implementation of the answers it generates, barring circumstantial interruptions (in other words, insofar as what you do depends on your desires as opposed to external forces, such as a sudden heart attack or meteoric impact). Let me now expand on these three points.

Ethics Is Hypothetical[8]

Immanuel Kant, as I noted in Chapter 1, taught us that morality is categorical, which is to say that, if something is morally right, then one is obligated to do it regardless of whether one wants to. Amorality, to the contrary, maintains that there is no such thing as obligation *tout court*, but only relative to something that one wants.[9] *This goes even for erstwhile moral injunctions.* For example, Kant argued that lying is wrong because it violates the categorical imperative to "Never treat anyone merely as a means." But an amoralist with Kantian leanings could arrive at the same practical conclusion by reasoning thus:

> If one wants to live in a Kantian manner, then one must never treat anyone merely as a means.
> Lying involves treating someone merely as a means.
> I want to live in a Kantian manner.
> Therefore I should not lie.

The conclusion of this argument is not categorical because it applies only contingently upon or relatively to my desire. That is the simple but crucial difference *in spirit* between morality and what I have been calling amorality.

I had originally been tempted to speak of "schmorality" instead of "morality" to indicate that amorality could be thought of as just like morality except that the absoluteness has been replaced by hypotheticalness. I felt that this humorous Yiddishism would be a sufficient check on any remaining moralistic tendencies. But now I feel that even a schmorality would be carrying too much moral baggage, for it still suggests that *something*—only now it's schmorality instead of morality—has pride of place in our practical reasoning. But I reject this suggestion.[10] In other words, I want to resist the moralistic inclination to imperialism in human decision making even if it were dressed up (or down) as schmorality.[11]

I see no need to suppose that every time somebody does something, it is ultimately due to some schmoral-theoretic motivation, such as wanting to treat all persons as ends in themselves (Kantianism) or wanting to maximize happiness in the world (eudaemonistic utilitarianism) . . . or even just wanting to maximize one's own happiness (eudaemonistic egoism). Far from it: On the vast majority of occasions, I venture to surmise, nothing of the sort is in mind, not even subconsciously. We have countless motivations and *types* of motivations, which move us in countless different types of circumstances; furthermore, different individuals will be responsive to a different (type of) motivation and/or combination of motivations in a given circumstance, and even oneself will be differently responsive to the same circumstance when in different moods and so on. The amoralist as such is simply not in the business of implementing a program the way the moralist is. The amoralist is just a desirer—or more specifically, on my account, one whose *considered* desires generate one's feelings or attitudes and motivate one's actions.[12]

Ethics Is Practical

Amorality, unlike morality, holds out the real hope of reaching conclusions about ethical issues. Consider this homely example. When I became a stepfather I suddenly faced mind-boggling issues which, at the time, I conceived as moral ones. For instance, as we all climbed into my new wife's car one day, I naturally headed for the passenger seat, but so did my tween stepson. Both of us had been used to occupying that seat, since theretofore we had never all been in my wife's/his mother's car at the same time. Now what? Well, I automatically conceived the question as a moral one; and it should come as no surprise, as my case against morality has made plain, that my moral conclusion coincided with my personal preference: *A spouse/parent should have pride of place in any family car.* I was not about to be treated like a child who sits in the back seat—and especially not when the person occupying the front seat would be another male.

But the nonsense, I now so clearly see, is that I was utterly conflating my gendered emotions with what was the right thing to do. Meanwhile my stepson was no doubt thinking something analogous, such as: "It's *not fair* that I should suddenly be relegated to the back seat because of this interloper in the family. I've been the man of the house these last few years and am not about to be demoted back to child status." And, again, had his mom just married another woman instead of a man, I doubt that my stepson's feelings would have been so strong about the "fairness" of the situation. What actually transpired thereupon was a semi-mock wrestling match between my stepson and me, since we were both quite serious and intent upon satisfying our respective but incompatible desires and also both enjoyed having a new playmate for some rough and tumble. I don't remember who won the match, but to this day I would not be able to resolve the *moral* question.

Thank God, I no longer feel I need to. It is so obvious to me now that there is no moral question, here or anywhere. Instead there is a purely practical question, and this much more promisingly suggests that there is a *correct* answer. Thus, instead of consulting my local moralist (which usually meant my own conscience) I would be better advised to write a letter to "Dear Abby" or some other agony aunt or uncle, who could draw on both folk wisdom and current psychological research for the best way to handle a situation such as this one. (If one were especially fortunate, one could turn to one's own parent for advice.) There are abundant empirical data and theory and just plain collected experience of the ages about parent/child relations, including the special cases of stepparent, male/male, preadolescent, and so on, and every combination thereof.

But in addition there is still ample room for a *bona fide ethicist* to chime in, for a crucial ingredient in the mix would be the question: What do I want, all things considered? That is because, even given all of the relevant knowledge about male stepfathers and male preadolescents, I would not have the foggiest idea about what to do, in the ethical sense I have defined, if I did not also know what I myself really wanted. For example, was it more important to me to be the alpha male in my new family than to have peaceable relations with my stepson?

On reflection it could have become apparent to me that I wanted both of these things with equal intensity and that both were at risk in this situation. In order to know my own mind, that is, my priority of desires, I would therefore have benefited from considering the relative risks to my family stature and to family harmony of my exercising presumed parental prerogatives on the one hand and acquiescing to my stepson's desires on the other. In the first case I could be seen as a bully, by both son and wife, whereas in the second I could come across as a wimp.[13] This recognition of a domestic Scylla and Charybdis might well have led me to steer a middle course of compromise: to suggest that my stepson and I take turns with the seating.

Further moving me in the direction of compromise would be a natural empathy with my stepson's aspirations, arising out of the above reflections on how *he* was viewing the situation. It is very common for us to condemn or seek to override another person precisely because we feel they have failed to empathize with *us*. Our own point of view and our own reasons are utterly salient in our own mind. Insofar as we consider ourselves to be rational and even respectful of the other, we might feel we had gone the extra mile if we had attempted to *explain* the virtues of our own position to the other. However, while it is indeed important in the pursuit of a mutually satisfactory resolution of a practical disagreement for the other person to understand where *you* are "coming from," this would still be only a self-centered enterprise if you did not also try, by means of dialogue or at least imagination, to bring the other's point of view and reasons into comparable salience with your own (that is, in *your* mind). Only then could a decision be made on the basis of the *total* relevant considerations.[14]

I should note that a moralist is likely to object that all I have done in the above illustration—of reasoning my way to a supposedly amoral conclusion—is arrive at the *morally* right decision. My having referred to my initial judgment—that I should always be the one to sit in the front seat—as the moral one was simply mistaken, argues the moralist; yes, it was a moral judgment, but it was the wrong moral judgment. It hardly follows that there is no (correct) moral judgment to be had. But my reply is my usual twofold one: There is no non-question-begging way to arrive at an authoritative categorical judgment in this case or any other, and the unintended consequences of thinking there is are baneful on balance.

Ethics Is Motivating

The central problem of normative ethics has been how to get from an *is* to an *ought*, for example, how to infer from the fact, or *is*, of someone's having lied, to the moral conclusion that they did something wrong (and so *ought* not to have done it). But I would say there is an equal problem in trying to go in the other direction: from an *ought* to an *is*. In fact this too is recognized by ethicists (albeit meta-ethicists): under the heading of "weakness of will." For it is a commonplace that a person can conclude or believe that s/he ought to do something and still does not do it, or that s/he ought not to do it but does it anyway.

The beauty of amorality is that it cuts right through both of these Gordian knots. There is no longer any problem of deriving an *ought* from an *is* because there is no more *ought* (in the moral, categorical sense) to be derived, and similarly for motivating moral behavior. In this chapter, moreover, I have been arguing that *ethics* (properly conceived) *does* have solutions to both of these problems (properly conceived). In the preceding section I illustrated how a desirist amoralist could indeed arrive at practical decisions. In the present section I shall argue that such decisions would *ipso facto* be motivating. My overall claim, then, is that amorality is the true ethics precisely because it is truly practical: It not only offers (a procedure for reaching) "answers" to questions like "How shall I live?" and "What shall I do, all things considered?" but also brings with it the motivation to so live and so do. The simple explanation is that amorality is based on desire (motivation), not on right and wrong. Thus, to paraphrase a move in Monopoly: Go directly to action and do not pass morality.[15]

A look at language will help me make my case. I have already forsworn the vocabulary of categorical morality, but I tentatively allowed the usage of hypothetical imperatives. Now I would like to go one step further and urge the elimination of even that (or at the very least advise extreme caution in their usage). Again my reason is the "moral baggage" that words like "should" and "ought" and "obligation" bring with them, even when couched in a relative or hypothetical context. They are so easily misunderstood, given our long history of using these terms absolutistically.

I would suggest a *substitution* for "should," namely "would." That is, the amoral sense of, for example, "I should never lie" is that I *would* ("in fact") never lie if, say, I ("truly") wanted more than anything else to live in a Kantian manner and I ("truly") believed that lying would frustrate that desire. This also gives us an empirical test of sincerity of desire (and/or belief); for somebody who claimed to believe that lying is anti-Kantian and to want more than anything to live like a Kantian, but who went around lying ad lib, would have some explaining to do.[16]

I could see giving up "should" and suchlike terminology in *all* normative contexts, not just the moral one. Thus, suppose a student in an English class asked the teacher, "Is it ever OK to use 'ain't'?" Instead of replying "You should never say 'ain't'"—which would make the teacher sound like a schoolmarm, in other words, a grammatical absolutist—the teacher could reply more precisely, "If you want to speak grammatically, then you should not (or just "don't") say 'ain't'." However, I think it would be ever better (and more literal) to say, "If you wanted to speak grammatically, you *would* not say 'ain't.'"[17]

This is not as big a deal in grammar as it is in ethics, however, since, typically, more hangs on the sort of decisions we are used to calling "ethical" than the sort we are used to calling "grammatical," as well as "aesthetic" and so forth. Also, we seem to be less "taken in" by the absolutist-sounding pronouncements of grammarians and aestheticians than by those of ethicists; for example, "beauty is in the eye of the beholder" is much less objectionable to the average ear than would be "(moral) rightness resides in the preference of the judge."[18] Therefore I am especially concerned to eliminate the language that all value systems hold in common from *ethics*-talk.[19]

To me all of this has been a liberation. To put it seemingly paradoxically, we are free because we are determined.[20] What I am getting at is that the hypothetical view of norms frees us from the tyranny of metaphysical absolutes, while at the same time subjecting us to the lawfulness of psychology.

This is captured by the notion of desirism I introduced in Chapter 3, which I characterized as "a metaphysical claim about the scope of human (or animal) motivation, namely, that it is restricted to the realm of natural causality." Thus, we are *free of* the need for a metaphysically *free will* that is responsive to the dictates of a metaphysical morality (not to mention a metaphysical grammaticality, etc.), because there are no such dictates, i.e., there is no metaphysical morality; we are off that hook, not weighed down by such a responsibility, immune to moral guilt. Instead, however, our every action is motivated by a desire, which is "determined" or caused like anything else in the empirical universe.[21]

I conclude that the answer to the ethical questions, "How shall I live?"[22] and "What shall I do?" is, "It depends on what you want."[23] By "what you want" I mean what you "*really*" want, that is, your net-desire after a reasonable amount of research and reflection on ends and means. If, all things considered, you want x, and y is the most congenial way to get it, then you *should* do y. In other (and I think less mischievous) words, if after due consideration you wanted x and you believed y was the most congenial way to get it, then, all other things equal, you *would* do y.[24] We could say: in lieu of prescription, prediction. This is the sum total of ethics. This is desirism. This is amorality.

A FINAL DEMUR

The moralist (who is actually my own doubting self) wants to make one final statement, as follows. Despite the effective parrying of the various objections to it, and its prior defense in Chapters 3 and 4, amorality remains a deeply troubling philosophy. I have been trying to put my mental finger on what is most disturbing—to identify the "baby" who seems to get discarded with the bath water. Now I think I know what it is: *the other*. Amorality seems solipsistic. The moralist grants that an amoralist could be filled with compassion. The problem is: This becomes a purely contingent affair. Nothing in the nature of ethics would require it. An individual amoralist could be an altruist, or an egoist, or a total jerk, for all ethics has to say in the matter. But does this not overlook the reality of "the other"? Is there not something about persons or sentient beings that *commands* a certain kind of regard and consideration and concern and respect? And is it not fundamental to morality, the very heart and soul of being moral, that we must pay attention to this feature of the other (and ultimately of ourself as well)?

In other words what I (as the *critic* of amorality) am suggesting is that equally essential to morality as its absolutism is its altruism—its lifting of the self out of its cocoon into a world of many selves. Both utilitarianism and Kantianism incorporate this feature into their moralities, albeit in very different ways. But although an individual amoralist could be utilitarian or

Kantian as a matter of motivation, the amoralist as such need not be either. An amoralist could, for instance, be utterly indifferent to the suffering of some fellow mortal, no matter how palpable and compelling that suffering might be to a more normally constituted human being. Amorality has no resources for ruling this out of bounds. Therefore, the moralist concludes, morality contributes something precious, priceless, to human affairs, which can in no way be replaced by nonmoral substitutes, not even compassion and altruism, if they are *merely recommended* rather than "commanded."

My reply (to myself!) is first to concede that there is a real loss in the relinquishment of morality. I personally experienced this full force, which, as noted in the Acknowledgments, was the inspiration of my prior manuscript on the subject: a memoir. It is painful to give up Santa Claus. It is painful to lose God. Illusions can be as powerful as reality, and so the loss of a treasured one can be as painful as the loss of something real. Indeed, amorality has often seemed to me like a dream, so "natural" and "real" had its moral opposite seemed to me. Perhaps I know this better than most, since I had been committed to morality not only implicitly like any other member of my society, but also explicitly as a professional ethicist of the Kantian variety. Furthermore, I was losing not only something that had seemed real to me, but that I had *valued* to the utmost. Finally, the particular sort of value it was had seemed to redound on *my own* value or worth as well; so that in giving it up I was almost ashamed (even though that could only represent a confused way of thinking at that point, like wondering what happened "before" the Big Bang; but I had not yet become accustomed to amoralist ways of conceptualizing my situation).

But that is part of "growing up," is it not? We lose our toys, we lose our parents, we lose our illusions—painful experiences all, but *sometimes* with compensating revelations.[25] I believe I have now found not only a viable but a satisfying substitute for morality. The saving graces are indeed the (purely contingent) compassion and Kantianism and suchlike that I still find flowering within me, no matter the loss of morality or perhaps even facilitated thereby. Granted, "gone" is the ironclad assurance that the universe somehow endorses these motivations. But what matters (to me), I see now, are the feelings themselves—the things I care about, and that I care about them (since I also care about my self-conception and my ideal of the world). So the fact that these feelings no longer rest on or testify to some metaphysical reality beyond themselves strikes me as the loss of exactly what *has* been lost, namely, *nothing*. All the metaphysics is unnecessary baggage—and worse than unnecessary, for it weighs us down with some very "heavy" matter indeed, such as anger, arrogance, intolerance, and all the rest.[26]

My advice to the anxious moralist is therefore this. If we truly care about "the other" (and, for that matter, ourselves) and hence desire that the world be filled with compassion, as well as other erstwhile moral desiderata, such as fairness and happiness, then *it is up to us* to cultivate them and to promulgate them.[27] There is no God to command it. There is no morality to justify it. *When you meet the Buddha on the road, kill him.*[28] There is only our desire for a certain kind of self and world. Absent that desire, no amount of (religious) preaching or (moral) argument will make the world as compassionate, etc., as it might be. Present the robust desire for such things, the preaching and the argumentation are at best superfluous and at worst get in the way. The only question, then, is whether the preaching and/or the argumentation might, in the run of cases, be necessary or helpful, that is, more helpful than not having them, to imbuing us with such a desire, given human psychology and circumstances. I don't *know* the answer, but I have given the reasons why I believe it is "No."

If we amoralists bring up our children as we were brought up by our moralist parents—to care about others, to appreciate them, to be motivated to help those who are in need, to be inhibited from hurting or deceiving anyone, etc.—should we not expect the same results? We all know the drill: drawing our wards' attention to the effects of their actions, pairing some of those actions with suitable rewards or punishments, and, high on the list, modeling in ourselves the behavior we desire in our children. But to think that this will be somehow ineffective because we neglected to punctuate all of these methods with moral language and mythology strikes me as odd— as odd as the religious claim that only the belief in eternal salvation could keep us from *molesting* our children.[29] I dare say an empirical study would not find an excess of child molesters among atheists. I venture to surmise the same would be true of amoralists.

Notes

NOTES TO THE INTRODUCTION

1. This becomes philosophy proper only when the adducing is done according to the canons of logic and subjected to critical scrutiny in dialogue.
2. Of course common knowledge, or any purported knowledge, can be contested. That is one of the two main items in question in any argument or dialogue: whether the premises are true. The other is whether the inference from the premises to the conclusion is valid or logical.
3. Joyce (2006) uses the same example.
4. The term "myth" comes from Joyce (2001); but although for Joyce morality is indeed a myth, it is not one he believes we should discard.
5. "Every writer in this volume adamantly affirms the objectivity of right and wrong" (Antony [2007], xii). Other prominent contemporary atheist moralists include Richard Dawkins (2006), Daniel Dennett (2006; also in Antony's volume), Greg Epstein (2009), Sam Harris (2010), and the late Christopher Hitchens (2007).
6. Ray Monk (1990) writes in his biography of Wittgenstein: "He took his examples . . . not from philosophers but from ordinary speech. And when he quoted from literature, it was not from the great philosophical works, nor from the philosophical journal *Mind*, but from Street & Smith's *Detective Story Magazine*" (p. 355).
7. " . . . not to let my thoughts be guided by anything but themselves," as Ludwig Wittgenstein put it in a letter to G. E. Moore (quoted in Monk [1990], 363). (I appreciate the irony of my citing someone else to reinforce my independence from other sources; but I am being consistent with my subsequent resolve to consign such references to a note.)

NOTES TO CHAPTER 1

1. From *Pippa Passes* by Robert Browning.
2. The latter pair are associated in Western ethics with Plato's *Euthyphro* dialogue.
3. Naming is not the same as judging since the latter implies knowledge while the former is merely discretionary. My "just as" refers only to our feeling impelled to categorize everything.
4. From Genesis 2 (King James Version).
5. Note that "this conception" is ambiguous since it could refer to morality as such or to a particular understanding of morality. I will consider both types

96 Notes to Chapter 1

of "conception" in this chapter. As I will explain, the respective inquiries are technically known as meta-ethics and normative ethics.

6. A new subdiscipline of philosophy known as "experimental philosophy" seeks to ascertain such things (Knobe and Nichols 2008). Hinckfuss (1987) had previously referred to this kind of investigation as "moral sociology."
7. Cf. Stich (2008): "I suspect that the practice of making moral judgments of the sort that Joyce [2006] describes is a culturally and temporally local one restricted to Western (and Western-influenced) cultural groups in relatively recent times."
8. Ultimately it becomes a substantive issue just whose (conception of) morality is in question since I will want to make the case that we would be better off without morality. But if my conception is not the most widespread one, then ridding ourselves of what is could be a mistake. Alternatively, if much of the world is innocent of morality to begin with, my claim would have correspondingly less import.

    A separate question is whether this book will be of interest to a given reader. The kind of morality I am characterizing in this chapter is no longer in vogue among professional philosophers. To them I would advise a detour to Chapter 5, where I give my reasons for rejecting the more modern conception of morality.
9. Strictly speaking, gravity does not act on us; but however contemporary physics would express our relation to it, gravity certainly would not leave it "up to us" whether we acted in accordance with it. Meanwhile, "willing" our actions is also, when you get down to it, an imprecise way of speaking. So a technical distinction is here being drawn in familiar language, but this should suffice since the distinction, once drawn, is an obvious one.
10. See Plato's *Euthyphro* dialogue.
11. The difference between your teacher and God is that the latter's pronouncements are infallible.
12. In Socrates' case (in Plato's *Euthyphro*), interestingly enough, it is a son's turning in his father for murder that is morally questioned despite its apparently having divine sanction.
13. An alternative strategy of theology has been to seek to vindicate a kind of guidance of human action that may at times diverge from morality. An outstanding example is Kierkegaard (1843).
14. This notion is from Kierkegaard (see, e.g., [1843] 1954, 69), although he, like me, asserts this only of the concept of morality and not of reality. However, Kierkegaard's reasons are the opposite of mine, he seeing God as "higher" still, whereas for me reality contains neither morality nor God.
15. McLeod (2001) calls this the overridingness thesis, which he critiques.
16. Strictly speaking, the opposite of *wrong* is not *right* but *not wrong*. The latter is the same as *permissible*, while the former is *obligatory*. So something which has been shown not to be wrong *could* be right, but has only been *shown* to be permissible.
17. The outstanding example in the West is the ethics of Immanuel Kant, as articulated in the *Grundlegung* (Kant 1785).
18. Note also that even if it turned out that something has color if and only if it has shape, so that neither property were ever found apart from the other, color and shape would still not be the same property. Just so, even if the moral and the rational never parted company, they would still be distinct notions. Morality is exemplified by a maxim like "Do unto others as you would have them do unto you." Rationality is exemplified by a rule like "*If p then q*, then *If -q then -p*."

Notes to Chapter 1

19. "Moral" is ambiguous in other ways as well, namely as the antonym of "immoral" ("Taking advantage of her in these circumstance would not be moral"; "moral" here means *morally permissible*), "nonmoral" ("This is an aesthetic question, not a moral one"; "moral" here means *pertaining to morality*), and "amoral" ("A sociopath lacks a moral sense"; "moral" here means *sensitive or responsive to moral distinctions*).
20. Cf.: "Irrational actions are those in which a man in some way defeats his own purposes, doing what is calculated to be disadvantageous or to frustrate his ends. Immorality does not *necessarily* involve any such thing" (Foot 1972, 310).
21. Cf.: "Now this principle of self-love or personal advantage may perhaps be quite compatible with one's entire future welfare, but the question is now whether it is right" (Kant [1785] 1993, 422).
22. One thinks of other ideal pairings: "Beauty is truth, truth beauty" (John Keats' *Ode on a Grecian Urn*) and "Whatever is, is right" (Alexander Pope's *Essay on Man*).
23. The late Philippa Foot referred very beautifully to the concept of morality we strive to elucidate as "the fugitive thought" (1972, 311).
24. The latter observation was made by Dr. R. T. Grant during the war (Monk 1990, 445–46).
25. Stich (1983) reminds us that our everyday or "folk" concepts "have a notoriously bad track record. Folk astronomy was false astronomy and not just in detail.... Much the same could be said for folk biology, folk chemistry, and folk physics" (p. 229). Stich's project is to build a case for the possibility of there being no such things as belief and desire, two staples of "folk psychology," in a mature science of the mind. This would in turn cast doubt on morality, my concern in this book; for "If we had to renounce folk psychology, we should probably have to reject the notions of personhood and moral agency as well" (p. 242). I am very much in sympathy with Stich's approach to the problem at hand, but my own will be more moderate although more direct. I will seek to discredit folk morality *by reliance on* folk psychology, albeit supplemented by scientific psychology. I do believe that ultimately folk psychology may bite the dust as well, but then, so might even (at least today's) scientific physics (since it contains unreconciled components, namely, relativity theory and quantum mechanics). My preference is therefore to move stepwise to ascertain how much of the familiar we can dispense with, without needing, not to mention being able (practically or intellectually) to dispense with all of it.
26. Cf. Aristotle in *Nicomachean Ethics*: "Our discussion will be adequate if it has as much clearness as the subject-matter admits of, for precision is not to be sought for alike in all discussions . . ." (bk. 1, ch. 3).
27. Or even just spend one's life squawking like a chicken.
28. The analogy extends further, for as mammals are a type of animal, morality is often considered to be a type of value—beauty being a typical other. (Thus, ethics and aesthetics are considered subdivisions of axiology, just as mammals and birds are both within the province of zoology.) Animals are in turn distinguished from plants and minerals as a type of things, while values are distinguished from facts as a type of truths.
29. Our physics could also be seen as manifesting it in its search for what it simply assumes awaits to be found, namely, a single explanation of everything. Cf. Cartwright's (1999) brief against the unity of science project.
30. Cf. Strawson's (1963) notion of "revisionary metaphysics."
31. It might be supposed that this constitutes an argument for there being such a thing as morality after all. For if there are definite constraints, despite some

98 Notes to Chapter 1

latitude, on what could ever be considered morally permissible, then doesn't this show it's not all in our head? Well, no, since it might only show that what's in our head is constrained. Compare: Maybe only women would ever be labeled witches because we have a definite conception of what a witch is; but this does not demonstrate that there are any witches at all. Furthermore, however, I am, recall, only describing my own conception of morality; alas for me, I have no assurance that even my strongest normative intuitions would be accepted by everyone else.

32. There is a trivial sense in which *everything* (subject to voluntary control) is a moral issue (according to the moralist), namely, as to whether it is at least permissible. This will become a significant matter, however, in relation to the argument for amorality (see the discussion of *schmorality* in Chapter 7).
33. Or we could say just "universal" both geographically and temporally.
34. The classic exposition is Mill (1861).
35. In the case of a tie, both are permissible and only their disjunction is obligatory.
36. The classic exposition is Kant (1785).
37. See Marks (2009).
38. The driver was also shortchanging his own value in some ways, for example, putting himself at risk as well; but at least that was done with his own end in view. If he had been treating himself with zero value, that too would count as wrong by the same criterion.
39. For a fuller exposition of this so-called Formula of Humanity interpretation of the categorical imperative, see Kant (1785, 4:429), and Marks (2009, 61–66).
40. Indeed, the growing *wealth* of Chinese society makes the ensuing argument even more compelling, as the toll on the *world's* resources could prove even higher than would have been the toll on China alone from a more entrenched poverty due to overpopulation.
41. For further explication see Marks (2009, 73–74).
42. To avoid terminological confusion it might make sense to give a different name to the normative categorical imperative. What makes matters even more confusing is that Kant offered at least three characterizations or formulations of it. He claimed that they all amounted to the same thing (Kant [1785], 4:421), but some of his interpreters have doubted this. Certainly on their face they appear to be distinct. However that may be, I have a favorite of the three, to wit: Always act in such a way that you treat persons as ends and never simply as means. This way of putting it also nicely brings out the crucial contrast to utilitarianism, which explicitly subordinates every kind of act, including the "treatment" of persons, as means to some ultimate end (for example, "the greatest good for the greatest number"). We could therefore call Kant's morality *respect for persons*, for it highlights, not the utility of our acts, but the regard for persons that they manifest.
43. Of course if one believed in a just God and eternal life, then prudent necessity could on some occasion counsel assuming some dire risk to one's worldly prospects. But in my example I am, as usual, speaking in the language of everyday concepts.
44. Keep in mind, of course, that the premise of the argument is itself an assertion, so the conclusion of the argument has not been proved unless or until the truth of the premise has been established.
45. Thus, an invalid argument is equivalent to an enthymematic valid argument. See Marks (1988) for a discussion of this seeming oddity.
46. In Chapter 5 I will say more about some alternative conceptions of morality, by way of rejecting them, in order to strengthen my case for there being no

such thing as morality (other than in thought). But, unless otherwise noted, my use of such terms as "the moralist" in this book refers to the type of morality I have sketched in this chapter.

NOTES TO CHAPTER 2

1. Strictly speaking, one need not be an amoralist just because one believes that morality is a myth. One could be, for example, a moral fictionalist, who believes that morality is a myth but nevertheless a useful myth, which we are therefore well advised to retain as a sort of pretense; see, e.g., Joyce (2001 and 2011). Like Garner (1994 and 2011), I will argue for full-blown amoralism in the sequel.
2. See, e.g., Sarkissian et al. (2011).
3. I believe the first assertion as well—that God does not exist—but it is not essential to my argument. It could, however, *follow from* my thesis, if God were understood, as He commonly is, as, by definition, a morally good being and/or the giver of morality (as opposed to, say, simply the Creator).
4. See Harman (1965) for an explication of this mode of argument.
5. This can be conceived as an inductive argument since the conclusion that *morality does not exist* does not follow with certainty. It does not follow with certainty because there is no way of knowing whether all of the current explanations on offer are exhaustive; so even if one were shown to be the best of the lot, another that is even better might show up a thousand years from now, or tomorrow. However, the argument could also be conceived as deductive if we took its conclusion to be only that *it is irrational to believe that* morality exists.
6. This is an empirical claim and, as such, has been contested by some experimental philosophers, e.g., Sarkissian et al. (2011). I am content to accept the non-universality of the assumption I have characterized and retreat to the claim that it is sufficiently extensive to make it of widespread interest and impact.
7. I must qualify this assertion with a very fat promissory note, since the details of such explanations and their empirical proofs are largely speculative. Thus, what I am actually asserting is that I myself find a certain sort of explanation to be eminently plausible, given the *Zeitgeist*. Perhaps useful comparisons would be the confidence (by the relevant communities) in Copernicanism and Darwinism well before their definitive empirical establishment.
8. Told to me by Mitchell Silver.
9. Indeed, I even believe that my belief that my belief that I am sitting at a computer etc. was caused by (or may even metaphysically *be*) some neurons in my brain firing, was *itself* caused by (or may even metaphysically *be*) some neurons in my brain firing ... and so on!
10. This is not the only ground for determining whether a belief constitutes *knowledge*: A true belief needs to have come about *in the right way* for it to be thus distinguished. Thus, if your only reason for believing that the earth is round was a dream you had, we would not say that you *knew* the earth was round.
11. This objection to Occam's Razor is in the same spirit as Socrates' expression of dissatisfaction with materialism:
    > It may be said, indeed, that without bones and muscles and the other parts of the body I cannot execute my purposes. But to say that I do as I do because of them, and that this is the way in which mind acts, and not from the choice of the best, is a very careless and idle mode

of speaking. I wonder that they cannot distinguish the cause from the condition, which the many, feeling about in the dark, are always mistaking and misnaming. (Plato 2001, para. 475)

12. Although, as noted in Chapter 1, even with a commander, the imperatives of morality would remain puzzling as having *moral authority*.
13. A common paraphrase of a passage from Dostoevsky's *The Brothers Karamazov* (bk. 2, ch. 6).
14. See Marks (2010a).
15. A theistic hard atheist is a *theist* who believes that without God, there would be no morality (but there is a God). I thank Richard Garner for pointing out the potential for confusion on this point. This is probably why the terminology of *compatibilism* is used in discussions of metaphysical determinism, to avoid an analogous linguistic confusion; thus, someone could be an indeterminist hard determinist, but less confusingly called an indeterminist incompatibilist. Similarly, I could speak of a theistic incompatibilist (or an incompatibilist theist).
16. This situation is analogous to Socrates' refutation of Euthyphro's theory of morality (or piety)—that the right thing to do is whatever the gods love—on the grounds that different gods love different things.
17. See Kant (1785).
18. Actually Kant's complete "story" trades on *three* metaphysical figments: freedom, immortality, and God. Including the two others would make it, then, an example of Explanation No. 1 instead of No. 2. My justification for omitting them is that Kant's ethics is commonly prized precisely for its (supposed) pure rationalism. This is most evident in the formulation of the categorical imperative that is based on universal law, and which Kant intends to be equivalent to the formulation of the Kingdom of Ends. It is therefore quite jarring to one who has only been exposed to Kant's moral theory in the *Grundlegung* (Kant 1785) to learn of his moral argument for God, which can be found in Chapter Two of the Transcendental Doctrine of Method in Kant 1781 and elsewhere. I leave all of this to the Kant scholars to hash out; see, e.g., the excellent discussion by Rossi (2009, secs. 3.2–3.5).
19. This epistemology is elaborated in Kant (1781).
20. Kant is fully aware of the problem, although he considers this awareness to be itself an accomplishment. In his characteristic way of expressing himself, he writes, "so even though we do not indeed grasp the practical unconditioned necessity of the moral imperative, we do nevertheless grasp its inconceivability" (conclusion of Kant [1785] 1993).
21. In the "West," anyway.
22. However, it would be unfair to characterize earlier generations of thinkers and scientists and laypersons as simple-minded. We more properly reserve that assessment for the denizens of today who persist in holding onto the old stories despite the advances that have been made in all fields of inquiry.
23. Kant (1785) 1993, 422.
24. And thus, contra Chapter 1, the moral would coincide with the rational after all.
25. See Kant (1799).
26. The appeal of Kant's test is that we do sometimes chastise a moral transgressor by saying, "What if everybody did that?" But in such cases we are not complaining that the immoral act would self-destruct; on the contrary, we are supposing that it would carry through successfully, but with undesirable consequences. For example, if lying were rampant, then people would become far more mistrustful than otherwise, and there would also be a heavy cost to society from efforts to circumvent lies, such as background checks, etc. (Of course this is exactly the world we live in.) This would not be a

Kantian objection to lying, but rather a utilitarian one (although, curiously, Kant sometimes seems to argue in just this way; see, e.g., Kant [1799] 1993, 426). Furthermore, it would not serve the meta-ethical purpose under discussion, for while it might explain why someone was *motivated* to inhibit and discourage lying, say, to prevent societal collapse, it does not explain why it would have been *wrong* for that person to lie, that is, even if he or she did not care that society might collapse.

An even more direct refutation of Kant's test is that a wrongful act can be universal and still effective. Consider for example the ubiquity of pricing things at x dollars "and 99 cents." This is a deceptive practice that presumably would not exist in a morally ideal world; yet it functions very well to achieve its aim of inducing people to purchase an item as if it cost x dollars and not x+1 dollars.

27. I owe this argument to Melanie Stengel.
28. This is why I was at first tempted to use Occam's Razor, you will recall, but concluded that inference to the best explanation made more sense.
29. The phrase comes from Leibniz (1710).
30. From James Boswell's *The Life of Samuel Johnson* (1791):
    After we came out of the church, we stood talking for some time together of Bishop Berkeley's ingenious sophistry to prove the nonexistence of matter, and that every thing in the universe is merely ideal. I observed, that though we are satisfied his doctrine is not true, it is impossible to refute it. I never shall forget the alacrity with which Johnson answered, striking his foot with mighty force against a large stone, till he rebounded from it—"I refute it *thus*."
31. But we should already be on our guard because person *has* been theologically laden, for example, as a being created "in the image of God" (Genesis 1:27, King James Version).
32. A recent example is Mills (2011). A different take on the pervasiveness of morality comes from Knobe (2010), who suggests that moral thinking is inextricably bound up with the rest of our human psychology, or as he puts it, "we are moralizing creatures through and through" (p. 328).
33. I have read popular accounts of general relativity that appear to interpret the furniture of the universe not as objects contained within it but as deformations of spacetime itself. *Whatever.*
34. I am not ruling out that our best theories will postulate or rely on more "ethereal" realities than spacetime and physical objects, such as forces, numbers, consciousness, and canons of reasoning. On the other hand, some of our current stock of concepts, such as beliefs and desires, could ultimately bite the dust; cf. Stich (1983). The sole metaphysical claim I am defending in this monograph is that *morality* is not required by our current best theories of reality.
35. Richard Joyce provides a concise summary on p. 52 of Joyce (2008). Freud (1927) is an obvious instance.
36. Cf. Foot (1972): "There is no difficulty about the idea that we feel we *have to* behave morally, and given the psychological conditions of the learning of moral behavior it is natural that we should have such feelings" (p. 312).
37. To paraphrase Thomas Aquinas on God in his *Summa Theologica* (1265–74).

NOTES TO CHAPTER 3

1. Socrates' (Plato's) concept from *Republic*, whereby the philosopher kings keep the populace deluded for the good of society.
2. As opposed even to a *make-believe* or "fictionalist" morality *à la* Joyce (2001 and 2011); see also Chapter 5.

3. I borrow the term from James (1903, ch. 8), to indicate the affirmative loss of an accustomed faith.
4. That desire can refer to something that is not itself a motivation is also clear from our ability to desire things that are not actions; for example, you can desire to be happy, or that tomorrow will be a sunny day, neither of which is something that you could *do*. Either could of course *figure in* a motivation, as when you are motivated (i.e., desire) to go for a hike because you desire to be happy (and know that hiking makes you happy). Cf. Marks (1986a).
5. This is not wholly faithful to Kant, since he based our moral judgment on reason and not conscience (Wood [forthcoming]). But as explained in Chapter 2, our moral functioning does contain something essentially metaphysical on the Kantian scheme, and will is the key.
6. On Kant's account the *good* will is "determined" by reason, but the very fact that there can be a bad or evil will proves that this sort of "determinism" is not causal or necessary. The Devil acted of his own free will; that is what made him the Devil. Had he merely been necessitated to act as he did, or due to some misunderstanding about what was rational, where would have been the evil?
7. There is a whole literature devoted to its analysis; see, e.g., Marks (1982 and 1986b) and Schroeder (2004).
8. Since the advent of experimental philosophy, all assertions of this sort must be taken with a grain of salt. I (and other philosophers) continue to make them, however, given the paucity of data currently available, which furthermore will be forever subject to interpretation, refinement, etc., in the manner of all social scientific research. Nevertheless I do not spurn experimental science but embrace it; it is only that I see it as a cautionary note or a corrective rather than a panacea or, *a fortiori*, a replacement for armchair philosophy. But neither does experimental philosophy itself take on such airs; e.g., "Experimentalists largely embrace traditional philosophical methods and simply seek to augment or revise these" (Phelan, forthcoming).
9. Haidt (2001) famously employs the same metaphor when making a pertinent claim about emotion and reason.
10. Additional discussion of this is included in the next chapter.
11. Not to say that this is unproblematic. For if morality is the highest *telos*, then intentionally to do something that one truly believed to be wrong would be to do something that one has decided, all things considered, one ought not to do. On the face of it this seems paradoxical. One might plead that one had not actually decided or intended to do what one did under these circumstances; for example, one may not have realized that one was hurting someone else, so while it was wrong to hurt the person, one only thought one was trying to cheer up the person. But there certainly do seem to be occasions when one is fully cognizant of both the wrongness of an action and the relevant description of what one is doing. In the philosophical literature this is sometimes called *akrasia* or "weakness of will," the relevant *will* being that faculty in us which has the power to respond to the moral law if we but exercised it.

Someone like Sartre ([1946] 1989) would claim, to the contrary, that we have no choice but to exercise our will—we cannot help but be free, as it were—and so there is no such thing as an ineffective will. Kant, too, would have to allow for a will that could act defiantly to the moral law, for, as previously noted, how else could there be a *bad* or *evil* will, or even a good will that was acting *freely*? But all of this is only what we would expect from the very notion of a moral law, which, as noted in Chapter 1, is precisely *not* like a law of nature that one has no choice but to "obey." The very essence of the moral "ought" is that, in full consciousness, one can disobey it.

Meanwhile, as an amoralist, I too believe that it is possible genuinely to believe that one morally ought to do x and still not do x; but the explanation I would give is that one would then be functioning under some impoverished notion of morality, such that it was *not* conceived as "what one should do all things considered," but rather something like "Society disapproves this" or "God will punish me for this." For it would indeed be a practical contradiction to do intentionally what one in full awareness at the time believed one ought *tout court* not to do.

Or so it seems. I would feel more confident about that if I had a parsing of the practical ought ready to hand. (More on this in Chapter 7.) But if it truly would be a contradiction to do what one believed one shouldn't, then a further implication is that a motivational desire can sometimes consist in a belief alone—namely, the belief that one *ought tout court* to do x—without a component desire of the inclinational sort. I thank William Lycan for alerting me to this objection that arose in his graduate seminar (personal communication 2008) to the thesis I defended in Marks (1986a).

12. Dennett (2006) makes this point with regard to theism.
13. See Broad (1952) and Butler (1726, sermons 1 and 11) for the classic analyses of egoism, which bring out this distinction.
14. This account can help to clarify what I mean by the subjectivity of value, for it does admit an objective element. In the example, *treating someone merely as a means* was understood to be an objective phenomenon. One could, for example, be *mistaken* about whether someone were doing such a thing to someone else; perhaps you thought I was treating someone merely as a means when you overheard me (supposedly) telling a lie to someone else, not realizing we were only rehearsing a play. But a moralist Kantian would *also* consider any *actual* instance of treating someone merely as a means to be *objectively* (*morally*) *wrong*. Such way of behaving, then, would be what *made* the behavior in question—for example, lying—wrong; it would be the *reason* it was wrong. An amoralist Kantian, such as myself, however, thinks that second type of attribution is *always* mistaken. Instead, the objective property of treating someone merely as a means would be what made the lie *distasteful* to me, the reason I *didn't like* it. Thus, for both the moralist and the amoralist there is some objective feature of the world that prompts our respective responses; but in the one case, the response is to make an additional objective attribution—of wrongness—while in the other, the response is simply itself—a subjective reaction of disliking. In other words, what the moralist thinks is wrong and what the amoralist dislikes could be one and the same objective feature of the world, in this case, that one person was treating another merely as a means.
15. See Marks (2009).
16. The long and the short of my objection to utilitarianism in Marks (2009) is that it is inconceivable that one could have the slightest idea which of all available options would yield the best overall consequences for all sentient beings into the indefinitely far future. See also Donagan (1979, sec. 6.5), Feldman (2006), and Lenman (2000).
17. "Spurn" as intellectually, not morally disreputable.
18. As mentioned in a previous note, this is a caution Dennett (2006) raised regarding the atheist's recommendations about religion.
19. E.g., Moeller (2009) concedes that morality may have played some important role in bringing about some welcome social institutions and innovations, such as law and civil rights, but contends that it is no longer needed and is now even counterproductive because "the times they are a-changin'" (p. 108).

104 Notes to Chapters 3 and 4

20. Indeed, as I suggested above, it is not even clear that humanity *has been* better off, by humanity's own lights, for there *having been* allegiance to morality rather than not. Maybe that was just a wrong turn from the start. I will take up this issue at greater length in the next chapter.

NOTES TO CHAPTER 4

1. Fish (2011) believes that philosophy in general stands indicted of this charge, "what I call the theory mistake, the mistake of thinking that your philosophical convictions (if you have them; most people don't) translate directly or even indirectly into the way you will act when you are not in a seminar." I quite disagree with Fish on this score because, concomitant with my acceptance of amorality has been the revelation that meta-ethics has tremendous practical import. That at any rate is what I hope to show in this chapter.
2. Of course we also value the flip side of moral worth, which is moral desert. Thus, while moral worth grounds the moral rights of its possessor, moral desert grounds her moral responsibility. The disappearance of moral desert from our worldview could also be experienced as a loss, since it would remove at least part of the basis of the satisfaction we feel when a wrongdoer or an evil person is punished. Cf. Moeller (2009, 55).
3. There is also of course negative value, or disvaluing something as *bad*.
4. Thus, note, my two main theses in this book are independent of each other; for my claim that *disbelief in morality might well be preferred by informed and reflective people* could be true even if my claim that *morality does not exist* were false. In this case I might be promoting a reverse Noble Lie (i.e., an Ignoble Lie)! (This would be analogous to the *deist* who argues that God exists but takes no interest in human affairs, and so, following Epicurus, we would be better off not even worrying about divine things. Thus, it is possible, although not my intention, that this book constitutes a defense, not of full-blown amorality, but only of an *amoral fictionalism*, turning the tables on moral fictionalism [to be discussed in Chapter 5] by arguing that we could be better off pretending that morality does not exist even though we know that it does.) Short of that, I will at least note that the main thesis of this book is so-called moral abolitionism, viz., that we might well be better off forsaking morality, i.e., dispensing with empirical morality (regardless of whether metaphysical morality exists), whereas the thesis that metaphysical morality does not exist (sometimes called "moral error theory" or "moral anti-realism") is just one consideration among many, and perhaps not an essential one, in favor of moral abolitionism.
5. As I explained in Marks (2009):
    I am not referring to the Baby Boom, although that too could be adduced, but more fundamentally to some plausible assumptions about human reproduction and personal identity. Since spermatozoa are as individualized as snowflakes, if someone so much as read a newspaper headline about *der Führer* (or was however indirectly affected later by someone who had), then, at a minimum, the moment of their offspring's conception was almost certainly different from what it otherwise would have been, hence also which sperm successfully penetrated the egg to become the male gamete, hence also the identity of the offspring. Therefore by, say, the year 2100, I surmise, and thenceforward till the end of time, every living human being will owe his or her existence to Hitler. But of course I should also say: to Hitler's grandparents, and even more to the point, to the woman who said *guten Morgen* to Hitler's grandmother

on that fateful day, thereby delaying grandmother's going to bed that night by one minute, and so on. (p. 42)
6. I ignore the even more perverse possibility that all alternative good-to-bad scenarios might have been even worse, i.e., even less to our liking. For example, it is frequently claimed that the carnage of conventional warfare that could well have resulted had the atomic bombing of Hiroshima and Nagasaki and then the arms race never occurred, would have far eclipsed in horror what has in fact occurred.
7. Although I could cite some relevant data. But as already suggested, the inability to clinch the case is as much a function of the state of human knowledge as it is of my professional proclivities.
8. Indeed, I could be mistaken even about whether I *have* become an amoralist, or at least amoral. Heaven knows I have friends who think that my (purported) amoral turn has only made me more moral(ist) than ever. More on this in Chapter 7.
9. I am forever indebted to Jesse Prinz (2007) for opening my eyes to this basic fact.
10. Of course one can also observe it in others, or study the relevant psychological science, or read literature, etc. But even though I had done all of that, it was only my becoming aware of my personal tendencies that finally persuaded me of the truth of the general thesis. And it is quite extraordinary how the utterly obvious can be completely hidden from oneself. But perhaps this does make sense with regard to awareness of one's own anger, since this kind of emotional state is precisely the sort wherein impartial inquiry, in this case into oneself, is most likely to be impeded.
11. See Marks (1982).
12. In this paragraph I am attempting to make conscious what Nietzsche asserts is always unconscious: "Gradually it has become clear to me what every [he says "great"] philosophy so far has been—namely, the personal confession of its author and a kind of involuntary and unconscious memoir . . ." (*Beyond Good and Evil*, trans. Walter Kaufman, [New York: Vintage, 1966], sec. 6). (He goes on to say, "the moral (or immoral) intentions in every philosophy constituted the real germ of life from which the whole plant had grown." This may be true in my case too, but only in the rejectionist way of speaking about morality that Nietzsche himself probably intended.) I thank Mitchell Silver for bringing this passage to my attention.
13. To paraphrase Squealer in George Orwell's *Animal Farm* (New York: Harcourt Brace Jovanovich, 1946).
14. Egoism and selfishness can themselves be distinguished, the latter being considered a short-sighted version of the former.
15. I have dubbed this phenomenon "moral pornography" (Marks 2011).
16. By the same token, this kind of motive gives one an incentive to magnify proverbial molehills into moral mountains. As I write, the most notorious item in the American news is Congressman Anthony Weiner's tweeting of photographs of his private parts to unsuspecting women. The amount of moral disgust this has generated is equal to anything I have ever witnessed regarding any event in the history of the world. If I were a moralist, I would find this *response* to be truly disgusting. The moralist chest beating and stone throwing and grandstanding are serving obvious political and personal ends of folks across the spectrum. As it is I am both amused and disappointed, and also motivated to rededicate myself to stamping out morality. For one thing, while Weiner has certainly behaved with supreme foolishness, that very behavior elicits from my personal heart a feeling of great sadness for his consequent suffering and also concern about the possible mental condition

that led him to do what he did (if it was not simply a manifestation of immaturity). For another thing, the welfare of his pregnant wife (not to mention, of their child to be) seems to be the last thing on the minds of the people who are supposedly protesting so vociferously on her behalf, since she is being put into an even worse position by the public reaction than she was by the original acts of her husband (hurtful as they surely were).

A different form of egotistic moral posturing, which, *mirabile dictu*, is even more patent, is to resent another's skepticism when one is telling them a lie. This has to be one of the more humorous human foibles, which I certainly know from my own possession of it. I have caught myself thinking/feeling, "How dare you doubt my honesty when I am deceiving you. I am an honest person!" To me this is a classic indication of the real functioning of morality.

17. See Milgram (1974).
18. And this, even though my dislike of egotism may be due to my having been raised to have a *moral* aversion to it. Does this mean that I dislike morality on moral grounds? No more, I would think, than the love of an adult for his or her mother reduces to the love of mother's milk that may have given rise to it in the first place. In philospeak: The intentional object of a desire is not always the same as the cause of the desire.
19. Well, we might throw in a little selfishness and ignorance as well.
20. Sometimes also the meaninglessness (or omnimeaningfulness) of moral phrases relegates them to the role of mere afterthought; thus, it is common to hear someone provide a long list of perfectly intelligible reasons for something and then end with, "And besides it's the right thing to do." A slightly more glorified role is to serve as a kind of punctuation, for example, ending a list of reasons with the, as it were, exclamation point, "And, *most importantly*, it's the right thing to do."
21. Thus, I could as well be writing a confession as a treatise . . . as indeed I have done (as part of the memoir mentioned in the Acknowledgments).
22. Indeed, they can become downright dangerous, a point Moeller (2009) makes very effectively in his discussion of the power of *just war theory* to facilitate waging war (p. 168). See also Hinckfuss (1987).
23. Intransigence is obviously often to be found on the employer's side too. In this book I tend to choose moralist examples from the "liberal" side of the political spectrum simply because I am trying to counteract my own moralism, which is liberally hued.
24. This gives me insight into what a wise counselor—the late Ron Mack—said to me many decades ago when I was despairing over a lost love: "It's only feelings." At the time I was confounded by this intended salve. *Only* feelings? Feelings were everything! But now at last I understand that, dammit, feelings are first and foremost feelings. Of course feelings can serve various functions that we care about and even be valued in themselves; but that is still a far cry from taking any given feeling at face value.
25. Throughout this book I use the term "desirable" (as also "preferable") in a relative sense, in other words, as meaning *desired* (by the relevant party or parties or group). I do this simply because it sounds better to my ear. This is one of those judgment calls—like the decision whether to retain empirical morality!—made in the face of conflicting considerations, in this case, that it could mislead or confuse the reader about whether I mean to attribute some objective quality to whatever I have designated as desirable. I don't.
26. Kekes (2011) is particularly good on this point.
27. This is precisely the kind of dissatisfaction Socrates had in the *Euthyphro* with divinity as the source of piety: the plurality of gods leaves us with no guidance because there is *too much* "guidance."

28. These two attitudes parallel the two "directions of fit" that are held to characterize belief and desire. See, e.g., Green (1991).
29. This assertion was surely inspired by Richard Posner's analogous one to Peter Singer in a debate on animal ethics, to wit: "And so to expand and invigorate the laws that protect animals will require not philosophical arguments . . . but facts, facts that will stimulate a greater empathetic response to animal suffering and facts that will alleviate concern about the human costs of further measures to reduce animal suffering" (Posner and Singer 2001). However, although Singer's defense of the value of moral argumentation is, in my opinion, demolished by Posner in their exchange, Singer does recognize more than Posner, I think, what is at stake, thus:
> Complete moral skepticism is, certainly, one way of meeting the ethical arguments I have made on behalf of animals, but it achieves that objective at a very high cost, because it means that you cannot make any other ethical arguments either, for example, against racism or homophobia in a society with deep-seated racist or homophobic moral intuitions that do not rest on any factual errors. Note that if you are really a skeptic about ethics, you must conclude not just that these arguments will be ineffective but also that there are no grounds for saying that the racists and homophobes are wrong. If you have to go to these lengths to resist my arguments for a new ethical status for animals, then at least as far as this exchange is concerned, I'm prepared to rest my case and hope that few readers will go along with your far-reaching skepticism about ethics.

30. This was a *Euthyphro* moment for me. In Plato's dialogue a crucial exchange between Socrates and the priest Euthyphro is when the philosopher asks, "Do you really believe these things [some of the stories about the Olympian gods] are true?" Euthyphro's unhesitating reply was, "Yes" (Plato 1981, 6b).
31. And I think it is not merely a coincidence that a few years previously I had been employed as a professional philosopher myself, while now I am retired and have had the leisure and "luxury" to ponder some of the fundamental assumptions of my own discipline. It is ironic to say the least that a professional philosopher hardly has the time to do what is most distinctly philosophical, namely, question a fundamental assumption. Or perhaps it is more a matter of "pressure" than lack of time, since a professional philosopher is expected to build a reputation in print and in speaking as the specialized defender of a particular point of view. But Socrates knew this, which is why he scoffed at the paid sophists and pursued his own vocation as an *amateur* or *lover* (*philo-*) of wisdom (*sophia*).
32. Therefore I would interpret the popularity of Mel Gibson's film, *The Passion of the Christ*, not as voyeuristic sadism but as projected moral masochism.
33. I think this criticism of the church can be found in Christianity itself. I see the parable of the sheep and the goats (Matthew 25:31–46) as the quintessential rebuke of those who place religious importance on anything else ahead of simple humanity (that is, kindness, etc.).
34. This is a theme to be found in Anscombe (1958). Pigden (1988) demurs.
35. Not even from a noumenal realm where my true self legislates itself, for all that is fantasy. (See Chapter 2.)
36. I happen to believe that there is no such thing as metaphysical free will since, as with metaphysical morality in Chapter 2, it has no place in the explanation of the universe I consider to be "best." (And, as with morality, it is not even clear that the notion is coherent.) But even if there were such a thing as free will, and bin Laden had been exercising it when making his decisions to murder thousands of citizens, I don't see why this need have *moral* implications.

Granted, a loss of faith in free will might undercut our retributive tendencies; cf. Greene and Cohen (2004). But if we were already convinced of amorality, then why would bin Laden's having freely chosen to murder civilians make us wish him to suffer or be treated disrespectfully in return (that is, over and above what it took to make him stop)? Instead of being caused largely by external factors beyond his control, he would have been wholly self-caused to do what he did—so what? There would still be no objective value attaching to his actions and motives; they would simply be different from ours, albeit dangerous to us. I could see that our *strategy* towards him might be affected; for example, if he were a metaphysically free being and had been captured alive, there would have been no point to try to rehabilitate him via a regime of causal reconditioning. But that still would not give us any noninstrumental reason to want him to suffer or be demeaned.

Meanwhile, no matter whether deterministically or voluntaristically considered, bin Laden's behavior and underlying beliefs and desires do not appear to differ in fundamental kind from those of persons considered by many Americans to be morally good. Lord knows there have been Presidents who have been widely respected despite their having authorized atrocities (e.g., the firebombing of Tokyo and the atom-bombing of Hiroshima and Nagasaki) or entertained potentially catastrophic religious ideas (e.g., Reagan's flirtation with Armageddon; see Dugger [1984]). And as I write, while President Obama is receiving universal praise from Americans (including myself) for his courage and wisdom in sending in the SEALs to capture or kill bin Laden, not a single American moralist voice, to my knowledge, has declared the alternative that was being urged upon Obama by some of his advisors—simply to bomb the residence into oblivion despite the known occupancy by many children and women and the uncertainty of bin Laden's presence (Drehle 2011)—to be unconscionable.

Finally, bin Laden's *aims*, apart from the religious mania, would seem difficult to find objectionable if they were as *Time* has articulated them. "Overthrowing the dictatorships and monarchies of the Middle East was long his central goal . . ." (Bergen 2011), and "The U.S. became a target because we supported the Arab autocracies" (Zakaria 2011).

37. Richard Garner is particular good on this subject in the chapters on applied ethics in the online revision of Garner (1994) at http://beyondmorality.com/beyond-beyond-morality/.
38. Or at least *aliefs*, to use the wonderful concept coined by Gendler (2008).
39. I owe this insight to David Koepsell (personal communication).
40. Cf. also Richard Dawkins' (2004) take on biological evolution: "My objection to supernatural beliefs is precisely that they miserably fail to do justice to the sublime grandeur of the real world" (p. 614).
41. A less commonplace case of re-visioning reality as interesting and indeed useful rather than moral is Richard Dawkins' (2007) decrying capital punishment on the ground that it denies us the opportunity to do research on what makes murderers tick.
42. A comprehensive edited volume on this subject is Statman (1993).
43. And even without morality I would still *want* to live in a society where people felt intrinsically inhibited about harming others and were thrown in jail if they did so frivolously or recklessly.
44. In other words, heed the Delphic injunction to *Know thyself*.
45. The police detective protagonist of the old TV crime show, *Dragnet*.
46. I credit Richard Garner (in personal communications) with impressing upon me this key insight. It is also spelled out with crystal clarity of illustrative detail in Zimmerman (1962).

47. I won't attempt to elucidate survival *of whom* or *what*: genes, the individual, the group, the species, the ecosystem? The general mechanism is all I require to make my point.
48. I recognize that I could just be a sucker to feel pity for Osama bin Laden in hiding. Would I be the sentencing judge who shows mercy to the defendant convicted of murdering his parents because now he is an orphan? Alternatively I could just be "projecting" some *self*-pity into bin Laden, rather than truly empathizing with him, since after all his could have been an utterly alien, and purely malign psychology. I suspect the truth lies somewhere in between. (See also the discussion of anthropomorphizing in Chapter 6.)
49. See the Acknowledgments.
50. See Chapter 5 for a discussion of moral fictionalism.
51. Indeed, so much to recommend it that, as noted previously, moral abolitionism might be able to hold its own *even if (metaphysical) morality existed*.
52. This is analogous to what I labeled "hard atheism" in Chapter 2. We might now refer to "hard moralism": the belief that without morality there is no ethics.
53. Granted, though, it could be rough going during the transitional period; so in order to motivate us to make the switch, we would need to find the value of empirical amorality to be not only greater than the value of empirical morality but also high enough to offset the cost of transitioning between the two. One thinks of the painful transition the United States underwent when the federal government shifted from a war budget to a welfare budget at the end of the Cold War. The state where I live was especially hurt, since Connecticut had the highest per capita investment in arms manufacture of any state in the union. But would this have been a good reason to rue the coming of peace between the superpowers?

NOTES TO CHAPTER 5

1. This is reminiscent of Armstrong's (1994) claim that one generation's atheism could be the next generation's theism.
2. This stratagem for retaining the trappings of morality while fundamentally revising its interpretation has been employed by much of the mainstream of modern ethics, from Hobbes through Hume and Hare and Harman to Haidt. All that I and like-minded *moral abolitionists* like Richard Garner are adding to this tradition is the finishing touch, or the *coup de grâce* delivered to morality. In other words: If it walks like a duck, quacks like a duck, and looks like a duck, then it must be a duck, or in this case, amorality.
3. Parfit (1984) offers an interesting discussion of the same question of whether to hold onto a given term when its referent undergoes fundamental change (pp. 472–73).
4. I am reminded of President George W. Bush's abrupt change of pretext for invading Iraq: from going after weapons of mass destruction to bringing democracy to the Mideast. But this was simply too big a switch *ex post facto* to constitute a legitimate rationale (at least in the eyes of most Democrats). Analogously, morality does not become legitimate just by stipulating its identity with something that might make more sense.
5. This argument exactly parallels that of Mitchell Silver (2006) regarding retention of the word "God" by the crop of "new theologians," who claim to be thoroughly rid of *Biblical* metaphysics.
6. This reaches the point of absurdity when the reality of morality is affirmed (if only by implication) and denied at the same time. For example, Haidt and

Kesebir (2010) offer a comprehensive analysis of "what morality really is," which they claim "is entirely descriptive . . ." and not to be confused with "what is really right or wrong" (p. 798). Yet their explanation of morality in exclusively empirical terms makes it bizarre to suppose that anything "*really is*" right or wrong; so by failing to repudiate that notion, they wind up in the same position as just about every other scientific or philosophic student of morality today, who go on assuming (or appearing to assume) that various things are right or wrong even as they analyze that concept out of existence. (Representative sources are too numerous to cite since this is the mainstream view, the mainstream schizophrenia, the mainstream incoherence.)

7. All of these terms have been given technical definitions in the philosophical literature, and, indeed, some of them have, confusingly, been given multiple definitions. Although I do indeed have that literature in mind, I will use the terms herein specifically to pick out a series of responses to desirist amorality.
8. I will take this as representative of moral desire, but recent work suggests that our moral psychology encompasses a variety of desires pertaining also to fairness, group membership, obedience to authority, and purity (Haidt and Kesebir 2010).
9. A simple and clear exposition of this sort of moral naturalism as part of a thoroughgoing naturalistic worldview is given by Clark (2012).
10. See his essay, *Of Cruelty*, in Montaigne (1580).
11. That is, external to our *empirical* minds, for Kantianism, as I recounted it in Chapter 2, does hinge on our having *metaphysical* minds, whose willing and reasoning are not themselves part of the causal nexus empirical science has revealed to us.
12. The whole quote: " . . . every particular person's pleasure and interest being different, 'tis impossible men cou'd ever agree in their sentiments and judgments, unless they chose some common point of view, from which they might survey their object, and which might cause it to appear the same to all of them" (Hume 1739, bk. 3, pt. 3, sec. 3). See also Cohon (2010, sec. 8).
13. The whole quote: "Celibacy, fasting, penance, mortification, self-denial, humility, silence, solitude, and the whole train of monkish virtues; for what reason are they everywhere rejected by men of sense, but because they serve no manner of purpose . . ." (Hume 1751, sec. 9). This statement is obviously tendentious and likely due to Hume's opposed personality as a *bon vivant* and his self-estimation as a "man of sense."
14. Some scholars may object to my characterization of Hume as a moralist. After all, he is commonly taken to have denied the possibility of deriving an *ought* from an *is* (Hume 1739, bk. 3, pt. 1, sec. 1), so how could he be offering a theory of morality in the sense of something truly authoritative in our lives? But Cohon (2010) points out that this is only one possible interpretation of Hume's famous observation and probably not the most plausible. Following on Cohon's lead, I understand Hume to have intended that only a *simple* or straightforward "derivation" will not suffice to support moral conclusions; for example, the deceptive aspect of a lie does not, in itself, make lying wrong. But the deceptive quality *in combination with* our aversion to deception (from the common point of view, of course) could move us to properly condemn lying as morally wrong.

Be that as it may, my aim in this section has only been to demonstrate the superiority of desirist amorality to any truly moralist constructivism, regardless of whether Humeanism is properly categorized as the latter. Furthermore, even if Hume was after all treating morality only as a phenomenon in need of analysis but having no special authority over our lives, he does not

appear ever to have advised therefore relegating moral language to the junk heap; whereas I do so advise, on grounds of its being misleadingly authoritative and thereby causing all kinds of mischief.
15. Cf. Wong (2006 and 2011).
16. "Wrong" here (and everywhere) is shorthand for wrong *in a particular circumstance*. So for example, in order for lying to be wrong, it need not be wrong as such (although it could be) but might be wrong only when intended to harm an innocent person. But even if lying were wrong only in that circumstance, it would be wrong *for anyone* to lie (in that circumstance).
17. As Sam Wheeler once put it (quoting from memory), "Everything I believe I believe to be true, and one of the things I believe is that some of my beliefs are false." This is the quintessence of rationality, it seems to me.
18. Cf. Boghossian (2011), who lays out a similar case against moral relativism, and clearly states the remaining options of moral absolutism and moral abolitionism, albeit balking at selecting the latter option.
19. Therefore they become in effect like the rabbi in the joke I recounted in Chapter 2.
20. That there is an implicit relativism even as to what constitutes the best explanation of the world, I must of course also admit. So in the end, as I have acknowledged from the beginning, I can only speak from my own subjective view of things. But there is also the possibility that at some point your and my subjectivities will agree. That is not necessarily the same thing as our both being "correct" even then, but it is nonetheless the best we could do, is it not?
21. This is the position of Richard Joyce and other so-called moral fictionalists. See Joyce (2001 and 2011).
22. For example, Joyce (2001) argues that moral beliefs, albeit false, "are a bulwark against the temptation of short-term profit" (p. 213).
23. I am indebted to Richard Garner for pressing this point upon me (personal communications).
24. I find that even when I start out to playact morality, as in a dialogue with a moralist opponent about an issue I care a lot about, I am in short order frothing at the mouth with moral contempt for and condemnation of my interlocutor because of the strength of my feelings and my decades of moralist habituation. Thus, I would say that moral fictionalism amounts to throwing out the baby but keeping the bath water.
25. Another comparison would be to conflate having emotions with being emotional. It is interesting therefore that both reason and emotion are claimed to have ersatz counterparts. This suggests perhaps a more fruitful avenue of criticism than simply pitting the one against the other wholesale (reason vs. emotion).
26. I will put aside the tricky question of how we would implement such a program. Socrates' (i.e., Plato's) solution in *Republic* for an analogous program was to confine the truth to a select few, who then imposed the lie on the general populace. This procedure seems implicitly undemocratic (and Plato makes no bones about his contempt for the *demos*). But it could also be downright unworkable, as I was suggesting in my discussion of fictionalism above. For the sake of the present discussion, however, I will grant that it could be done; after all, human beings do seem to possess a remarkable ability to live not only with false beliefs but outright contradictions.
27. Thus, I am *not* alluding to the common observation that we can never really *know* the springs of our behavior. Cf. Kant (1785, 4:407).
28. It is difficult even to articulate what is at issue here because of the ambiguity of the words "moralism" and "moralist" and "moralistic." These terms

can refer, depending on context, either in the pejorative sense (self-righteous, etc.) or in the straightforward sense (believes in right and wrong). Since I myself am highly skeptical that there is much of a difference between the two types of moralism in actual practice, I will, having given my reply to the present objection, simply continue not to worry much about the ambiguity in my usage of the words in this work.

29. I offer this as a friendly criticism of Kekes (2011), which I think could be successfully reworked as an indictment of morality and not just of being moralistic.
30. In other words, sometimes the very power of a weapon is what makes us want to relinquish it. Think of MAD (i.e., mutual deterrence by threat of mutually assured destruction with nuclear weapons).
31. Events have caught up with me as I wrote that sentence. See Global Commission (2011).
32. But I will give a more respectful, final hearing to the Baby and the Bath Water Objection at the very end of this book.

NOTES TO CHAPTER 6

1. From here on, "animals" for short.
2. There is a huge literature on this sorry subject, but one need only consult the classic contemporary source: Singer (1975).
3. The precise number is hard to peg, although conservative data are available; see, e.g., http://www.upc-online.org/slaughter/2000slaughter_stats.html. But a back-of-the-envelope calculation is enough to show that killing on average, say, ten chickens to feed each human being per annum already brings the total to 70 billion sentient beings. If fish are included in the total, then Americans alone kill and eat that many animals; see, e.g., http://www.animalliberationfront.com/Practical/FactoryFarm/USDAnumbers.htm.
4. Regarding human nutrition and health, consider this position statement by the American Dietetic Association (2009): " . . . appropriately planned vegetarian diets, including total vegetarian or vegan diets, are healthful, nutritionally adequate, and may provide health benefits in the prevention and treatment of certain diseases" (p. 1277). Regarding the effect of animal agriculture on the environment, consider this from the Food and Agriculture Organization of the United Nations: "the livestock sector generates more greenhouse gas emissions as measured in CO_2 equivalent—18 percent—than transport. It is also a major source of land and water degradation" (Matthews 2006).
5. Peter Carruthers is notorious among contemporary thinkers for espousing this view (see, e.g., Carruthers [1992]), although he has hedged and revised his conclusions over time (see, e.g., Carruthers [1999]). I do not mean to demean the sophistication of his argumentation; I even agree with a lot of it. But I am not alone in finding his denial of conscious experience to most and possibly all nonhuman animals to be absurd on its face. For a reasoned rebuttal of Carruthers on this point see Lurz (2002, sec. 3.2).
6. More precisely, the usual argument is that nonhuman animals lack the cognitive capacity to envision and plan their future existence in the explicit manner that human beings do. But it would be an equivocation to infer from their having no conscious interest in their future existence to their not having an interest, i.e., a stake, in their future existence. For example, presumably they have a stake in possible future pleasurable experiences that being killed would preclude. Cf. Francione (2000, 137), and Yeates (2010).

7. Unlike the two preceding, this claim is true; but I still maintain that the argument that contains it as a premise is laughable because the presumption is that human beings *do* have immortal souls. However, even someone who takes the religious metaphysics seriously can deny that animals' lacking an immortal soul is a good ground for doing with them as we please; see, e.g., Linzey (2009, 25–27).
8. As the immediately preceding notes reveal, I recognize that this remark is intemperate, not to mention, false. While I do believe that such motives are pervasive (if often unaware), the more apt observation is that the arguments they motivate are easily refuted. In any case, the meat (or tofu) of my argument for amorality is in the refutation of the moral arguments *against* factory farming (etc.), which follows.
9. The latter position is the so-called abolitionist one, according to which the breeding of domestic animals would cease and the preservation of natural habitats for wild animals become our sole commerce with the nonhuman sentient world. See, e.g., Hall (2010).
10. Cf. Lee Hall's (2006) assertion that "It's simply not plausible that humanity can renounce our privileged position over [other animals], yet live in situations where we *could* exert our will" (p. 53).
11. This is analogous to the argument that slavery should be abolished as a massive scourge even though there are no doubt instances, perhaps many, when slaves are well treated by their masters.
12. For example, according to the Humane Society of the United States (2009) millions of dogs and cats are euthanized by shelters in the United States every year.
13. I am talking here about the theoretical sense of "working": Is there a sound moral argument for condemning all use of animals? But there is also a pragmatic sense of "working": Is there a moral argument, sound or unsound, that will move people to stop using animals? There is a growing cadre of animal activists who defend a "No" answer to the second question; see, e.g., Cooney (2011) and Fetissenko (2011). I also address this issue as the chapter proceeds.
14. By coincidence "abolitionism" is a name for both the position in animal ethics I am defending in this chapter and the position on empirical morality I am defending in this book.
15. I take this terminology—"let alone" and "on their own terms"—from Catharine MacKinnon (2004) and Lee Hall (2010), respectively (although neither author is arguing from a utilitarian position).
16. For example: "life, however valuable in itself, can only be sustained by care in relationships" (Gilligan 1982, 127).
17. "When we try to pick anything out by itself, we find it hitched to everything else in the universe" (Muir [1911] 1998, 110).
18. McMahan (2008) puts the argument for "benign carnivorism" through its paces.
19. For discussion of this distinction see Marks (2008).
20. This is the mainstream position of most animal advocacy organizations, such as the Humane Society of the United States. There is also a third form of animal welfarism, which stresses it as effective strategy towards achieving abolitionist ends; Robert Garner seems to hold such a position, as portrayed (and vehemently disputed by Gary Francione) in Francione and Garner (2010).
21. Thus, the form of the rights claim is analogous to that of the welfare claim, since the latter also attributes a feature in common to all who merit moral consideration, typically, sentience, the capacity to experience, at a minimum, pain or suffering.

22. I myself, when still a moralist, had argued for inherent rights on a different basis, namely, the capacity to value something. See Marks (2009, ch. 5).
23. Of course there are some conditions under which even human beings lack this power, such as in infancy or in a coma.
24. Cf. Bekoff and Pierce (2009) on the morally relevant capacities of other animals.
25. For example, this acknowledgment from a *supporter* of animal experimentation: "If voluntary consent were our standard for animal research, the whole business would end—not because we cannot understand what the animals are telling us, but because we can" (Carbone 2004, 179).
26. See Marks (2009, ch. 4).
27. For example: "It's a fact of life on Earth as well as a strain on the advocate's emotions that the world's animals [that is, wild animals living freely in their natural habitats] often have short, stressful lives" (Hall 2010, 172). But therefore to a person such as Hall or myself, the prospect held out by some utilitarians of eliminating natural predators from the wild, should it turn out that by doing so we would achieve less pain in the world, seems truly bizarre. McMahan (2010), for one, ponders such a scenario. (And yet, I must admit that all that really stands in my own way of accepting such a suggestion is a *romantic* view of the natural world—a picture in my own mind that I simply find attractive.)
28. Smith (1965, 106).
29. Hall (2006) was an inspiration for this idea.
30. It is in fact impossible to refrain completely from using other animals, which is to say in the lingo, to be a pure *vegan*. Humanity has shown an efficiency in its use of animals that could be viewed as a virtue by a moralist who did not care about them . . . or was not haunted by the image of lampshades being made from the skin of concentration camp inmates (Jacobson 2010). Waste has been reduced to a minimum by finding every conceivable way to insinuate the parts of slaughtered animals into the human world (see, e.g., Mottershead [2011]). Will future vegans even have to give up driving because the new fuels will contain rendered fat from slaughterhouses? (See Krauss [2007] on this development.) This sort of thing creates agonizing choices for moralist vegans; consider, e.g., Gary Steiner (2009).
31. An even easier and far more common "out" is bad faith, in this case exemplified by those who suspect that meat eating is morally problematic *and therefore* they just don't think about it. (I thank Mitchell Silver for telling me about his encounter with this phenomenon.) Related to this would be the Chinese philosopher Mencius' advice to King Hui of Liang: "When it comes to animals, if the Superior Man has seen them while alive, he cannot stand to watch them die. If he hears their screams, he cannot stand to eat their meat. Therefore he stays away from the kitchen" (Mencius 1A:7).

    Meanwhile, a third moral philosopher of my acquaintance, when asked about the apparent contradiction between his expressed concern about the animal plight and his carnivorous eating habits, denied suffering from either weakness of will or bad faith but elucidated his moral justification only by remarking that "It's complicated." To me this is a red flag. Or is it a white flag?

    I must finally express my overall amazement and disappointment at the lengths of silliness to which grown (and highly educated and otherwise sophisticated and mature) men and women are capable of going—and *do* go in the vast majority of cases—to defend a trivial prerogative over what they themselves would style a moral imperative (not to mention, one of the greatest magnitude). "What, shall we stop eating at all? Maybe plants have feelings too!"—etc. ad inf. It is as if they felt they were being asked to sacrifice their firstborn rather than simply to alter their eating habits (not to mention, in order to prevent untold atrocities). My personal journey of animal activism has enabled me to peer through a window into the soul of the inner child(ishness) of humanity. Cf.: "A story is told of an old priest, who, asked if he had learned anything about human beings in his many years of hearing confessions, first said 'No,' but then, 'Yes. There are no grown-ups'" (Foot 2001, 108).

32. Although veganism has come to connote abstinence from all, and not only dietary animal use, I am convinced by the argument that dietary veganism makes sense as the main strategy for animal liberation: both because it accounts for the vast majority of animal (ab)use and because the boycotting of food made from animals would inevitably exert both social and economic pressure on every other kind of use of animals.

33. Some animal ethicists caution that the eating of animals has far greater significance in human life than mere habitual gustatory preference (see, e.g., Ciocchetti [Forthcoming]). The authors are typically making a moral case for vegetarianism and still believe that the arguments favor their position. Similarly I believe that, despite the obvious cultural significance of eating animals, other nonmoral considerations for *not* doing so would attain motivational ascendency among those who were able to reflect on all of the relevant information.

34. See for yourself: http://www.youtube.com/watch?v=JJ—faib7to&list=PLEC1AB61BABE96E13&index=3&feature=plpp_video (accessed April 9, 2012).

35. Cf.:
> Animals are drowned, suffocated, and starved to death; they have their limbs severed and their organs crushed; they are burned, exposed to radiation, and used in experimental surgeries; they are shocked, raised in isolation, exposed to weapons of mass destruction, and rendered blind or paralyzed; they are given heart attacks, ulcers, paralysis, and seizures; they are forced to inhale tobacco smoke, drink alcohol, and ingest various drugs, such as heroine [sic] and cocaine.
>
> And they say ARAs [animal rights activists] are violent. The bitter truth would be laughable if it were not so tragic (Regan [2004, 235]; in the article, however, Regan comes out *against* the use of violence to promote animal ethics).

36. Indeed, an irony for me is to read the *Guidelines* of the Animal Liberation Front reprinted in Best and Nocella (2004, 8), and be philosophically puzzled about why they appear to limit "direct action" to action that does not harm a human being. Such a limitation does not seem to me to be consistent with the implications of some of the moral arguments presented for direct action in that same volume.

Meanwhile there are some animal advocates who attempt to provide an explicit theoretical framework of nonviolence for the animal movement; consider, e.g., Lee Hall (2006).

I should also point out that very little extreme violence—or some would say violence *simpliciter*—has in fact been committed by animal activists. I only mean to be discussing the emotional attitudes and argumentative logic that seem to me to be concomitant with moralist animal advocacy.

Finally, I do need to clarify that there is also a significant "middle ground" between respectful dialogue and extreme tactics like threatening, arson, and violence. I have in mind such actions as surreptitiously videotaping the conditions inside animal industries.

37. I picture Charlton Heston at the end of the movie, *Beneath the Planet of the Apes*, who becomes so disgusted at what humanity has become that he literally destroys the whole world.
38. Cf. what happens when someone takes the red pill in *The Matrix*.
39. A prior objection would be that I have erroneously equated (almost-)universal moral condemnation with misanthropy. Hall (2006), for example, argues that the animal advocate's concern about nonhuman animals is at base a concern about animals, humans included, and so we would want to cultivate universal respect and compassion for human beings as well as for animals. However, recall my reply to the objection of moralizing in Chapter 5, where I argued that we must not mistake a concept for reality. My claim in the present argument is that moralist thinking about animal ethics would, *as a matter of empirical likelihood*, stoke misanthropy.
40. The term was coined by psychologist Richard Ryder, who recounts its history here: http://www.richardryder.co.uk/speciesism.html (accessed April 9, 2012).
41. On the other hand, it could well be that the proper way to understand speciesism is as a form of moralism, for example, as the view that nonhuman species have inherently less worth than the human species simply in virtue of not being human. In that case I am not speciesist at all, and for two reasons: (1) I don't believe there is such a thing as inherent worth and (2) If I did, I would probably attribute equal inherent worth to all sentient beings in virtue of their adaptation (and hence relativized intelligence, sensitivity, etc.) to their respective ecological niches. But even in the latter case, moralists recognize preferential treatment, for example, of one's own children over other people's in certain situations, despite there being no question of other children having less inherent worth than one's own.
42. In Marks (2010b, 110–11), I provide an example where I think all human beings would be speciesist (in the sense of showing a preference for our own species), although I cannot rule out that there could be some people who would act in a way that I would not, by my own psychology, be able to fathom. Indeed, I cannot even predict whether I myself might eventually "come around" to the extirpation of speciesism from my soul. Meanwhile, much ink has been spilled by both Singerians and Reganites over the question of whether, if somebody must be thrown out of a lifeboat to save the rest, it should be the dog rather than any of the human occupants (or nobody). As always I believe there is no "should" about it; I am only interested in what people *would* do if fully informed and reflective.
43. It has also been argued that the kind of respectful activism I prefer is given a leg up precisely by being able to contrast itself to the more violent alternatives. Did animal users not fear the latter, they would not give a warm hearing to the former. On this view, then, the more extreme tactics are not intended to bring about the overthrow of animal use directly, but only indirectly by facilitating the work of the "middle." To which I can only reply: I don't know if that's how things work, but thanks but no thanks.
44. See Hadley (2009).
45. See Braithwaite (2010).
46. High on my list would be books like Marc Bekoff (2007), Karen Davis (2009), and Jonathan Balcombe (2006).
47. It would be hard to beat Tribe of Heart's documentary, *Peaceable Kingdom: The Journey Home*, for insight into the lives of farm animals.
48. "What is the secret of soylent green?" as the trailer of this 1973 science fiction movie asks. I won't spoil it for you.

49. For example, here is a comprehensive interactive map of where animal abuse has been videotaped: http://www.animalvisuals.org/projects/data/investigations (accessed April 9, 2012).
50. A most interesting and effective organization in this regard is Vegan Outreach, which focuses almost entirely on handing out brochures to college students.
51. Large organizations like PETA have staffed departments for researching the published literature of animal farming and experimentation, and several organizations of all sizes support surreptitious documentation of animal use in industries that conceal their activities.
52. For example, Carbone (2004), Singer and Mason (2006), and Davis (2009).
53. Fetissenko (2011) argues that this is the appeal most likely to influence people. I agree with his de-emphasis on moralist rhetoric but am far from reconciled to his equal de-emphasis on "emotional appeals" (p. 150), that is, appeals to altruism and compassion. Of course he is right to see these questions as empirical ones (p. 163). His evidence of effectiveness is mainly historical, mine phenomenological.
54. An excellent review can be found in Engel (2000).
55. See Matthews (2006).
56. See Ilea (2009) for a comprehensive review of environmental damage by animal agriculture.
57. From Diamond (2002):
    The main killers of humans since the advent of agriculture have been acute, highly infectious, epidemic diseases that are confined to humans and that either kill the victim quickly or, if the victim recovers, immunize him/her for life. . . . The mystery of the origins of many of these diseases has been solved by molecular biological studies of recent decades, demonstrating that they evolved from similar epidemic diseases of our herd domestic animals with which we began to come into close contact 10,000 years ago. (p. 703)
58. See, e.g., Katz (2011).
59. For example:
    The results of an evidence-based review showed that a vegetarian diet is associated with a lower risk of death from ischemic heart disease. Vegetarians also appear to have lower low-density lipoprotein cholesterol levels, lower blood pressure, and lower rates of hypertension and type 2 diabetes than nonvegetarians. Furthermore, vegetarians tend to have a lower body mass index and lower overall cancer rates. (American Dietetic Association 2009, 1266)
60. According to the Pew Campaign on Human Health and Industrial Farming (2012):
    . . . antibiotics often are used on industrial farms not only to treat sick animals but also to offset crowding and poor sanitation, as well as to spur animal growth. *In fact, up to 70 percent of all antibiotics sold in the U.S. are given to healthy food animals.*
    The U.S. Food and Drug Administration, U.S. Department of Agriculture and the CDC testified before Congress that there was a definitive link between the routine, non-therapeutic uses of antibiotics in food animal production and the crisis of antibiotic resistance in humans. Moreover, the American Medical Association, the American Academy of Pediatrics and other leading medical groups all warn that the routine use of antibiotics in food animals presents a serious and growing threat to human health because it creates new strains of

118   Notes to Chapters 6 and 7

dangerous antibiotic-resistant bacteria. (emphasis in original and citing Mellon et al. [2001])

61. Thus, what I am proposing is a variant of Richard Brandt's (1979) notion of cognitive psychotherapy. It is a *variant* because Brandt was concerned with establishing what is objectively good whereas I mean only to assert my preferred means of establishing what to do.
62. In this I follow people like Gary Francione (2012) and Lee Hall (2010) (*sans* their moralism).
63. I have tried to demonstrate how easy it is to be(come) vegan with a website I have created, aptly called TheEasyVegan.com.
64. A recent entry in this field is Scruton (2006, 61–3).
65. Hence I completely concur with Gary Francione (2009) that what is sought is "a revolution of the heart."
66. A moralist could claim that I am simply modeling a less moralistic way of inculcating moral behavior. I have dealt with this general objection to the amoralist project in Chapter 5.
67. A case in point is Time.com food columnist Josh Ozersky, who writes (2011):
    . . . I get the point made by animal-rights activists. Their primary arguments (that eating other animals is unnecessary, that their lives are as valuable as ours, that eating meat has catastrophic effects on our environment) are, to be honest, unanswerable. I admit that. I just don't want to stop eating meat. In fact, I want to eat even more of it than I do, if that's possible. But you won't hear me making bumper-sticker arguments like: "If God wanted us to eat lettuce, he wouldn't have given us teeth." Like my hero Tony Soprano, I understand there are certain moral realities in my life that I just have to make my peace with. And my peace rests on this side of pork chops.

NOTES TO CHAPTER 7

1. A general statement and defense of this type of objection is given in Kramer (2009).
2. At the opening of his *Introduction to Logic* (New York: Macmillan, 1982), Irving M. Copi quotes the following passage from the *Discourses* of Epictetus:
    When one of his audience said, "Convince me that logic is useful," he said,
    Would you have me demonstrate it?
    "Yes."
    Well, then, must I not use a demonstrative argument?
    And, when the other agreed, he said, How then shall you know if I impose upon you? And when the man had no answer, he said, You see how you yourself admit that logic is necessary, if without it you are not even able to learn this much—whether it is necessary or not.
3. Maybe a still more apt comparison is with the condition of mathematician John Nash at the end of the fictionalized biographic film *A Beautiful Mind*, who is able to manage his schizophrenia, but only by contending against lifelike hallucinatory temptations. For morality is a powerful delusion indeed. I do not doubt, therefore, that some of my readers will see me as "crazy" precisely for attempting to *shake off* what I am now characterizing as a delusion; for the proper interpretation of the strength of morality's pull on us, we usually believe, is that it is something *real*. My own experience has undergone a 180-degree Gestalt shift in this regard, however, such that it is precisely the

strength of my moral intuitions that reveals to me that they are fundamentally *feelings* rather than intimations of truth.
4. Pizarro (2011) offers a concise defense of a notion he dubs "stubborn moralism," according to which our moralist responses may be so "hard-wired" (p. 1) as to be irresistible. And this is the case even though they may be based on false belief, because of the evolutionary advantage they have given to us. I am very sympathetic to this position. I would reply, however, that today we may have better reasons, as explained in Chapter 4, for resisting, difficult as this may be. And if indeed resistance is futile (quoth the Borg in Star Trek), except possibly for some mutants (such as myself?!), then someday it might be accomplished by genetic engineers who have been convinced by my arguments. (This would seem to run counter to the current enthusiasm by some "transhumanists" for making us even *more* moral, on which see Douglas [2008]; but of course as always whether we are really at odds depends on how "moral" is being understood.)
5. That is, immoral in the eyes of the moralist hypocrite. In my eyes it would be, like all behavior, simply nonmoral.
6. Granted, Person A is not strictly speaking being hypocritical or deceptive if she genuinely believes that there is such a thing as morality. So then I would simply locate my criticism beneath a different rubric.
7. When I say I "just don't like" something, I do not mean to suggest that there is no story to be told. As with everything else in the empirical universe, there is presumably a causal explanation. The import of the phrase, then, is only that there are cases where the causal story is unknown (and/or of no interest) to us, and so our desire appears to be "brute." But there is surely nothing mysterious about the explanation in the present example; my aversion to unfairness probably has to do with both a genetic predisposition, as a dislike of unfairness seems widespread in the human and indeed animal (see Bekoff and Pierce [2009]) population and easily understood in evolutionary terms, and my upbringing and education.
8. This is essentially the thesis of Foot (1972). However, Foot retained the label of "morality," offering simply a different analysis of the phenomenon in question. I have given my reasons for taking the extra step to moral abolitionism. (Foot more recently [2001] defended a non-hypothetical basis for morality in practical rationality, which I view as a step backward.)
9. I shall argue below, in the section "Ethics is motivating," that *obligation* drops out altogether.
10. Indeed, I reject it even for morality. For example, I do not think that even a moralist need insist that whether to use red or green to paint a shadow in a landscape is a moral matter, not even as regards its (moral) permissibility. It is (other things equal) a *purely* aesthetic decision. Kekes (2011) makes this sort of point. And thus, I reject Mitchell Silver's (2011) characterization of moral rules as those which "classify all possible actions as permissible or impermissible" (p. 21).
11. Joyce (2008) uses the term "schmorality" to pick out failed *candidates* for morality that bear a close resemblance to morality but lack some essential feature or fail to serve some function that morality has importantly played in human existence. He uses it to denigrate those candidates. My original use of the term was to label something that I *would* put forward as a *substitute* for morality. But it was also a schmorality in Joyce's sense since it clearly lacked something that would make it a morality. Now, however, I reject the term and the concept as helpful even for amoral purposes.
12. More precisely I might say that the amoralist is just a practical reasoner. So there *is* a "program," namely, to be rational, i.e., to decide things on the

basis of a reasonable amount of critical research and reflection on relevant information; but it is not a *special* program distinct from that.

13. Yet another variable to consider would be the manner in which I strove to resolve the problem, for example: by parental fiat or by discussion with stepson or with wife/mother or both together? Indeed the manner of resolution could loom larger in the fulfillment of my desires than the particular resolution arrived at.
14. For a decade I wrote a column for *Philosophy Now* magazine called "Moral Moments," wherein I would dissect practical problems of just this sort and suggest my own moral resolutions of them. Upon my amoral awakening, I debated with myself whether to change the name of the column to "Amoral Moments," but finally decided on "Ethical Episodes." The present analysis is a perfect example of an amoral moment.
15. Richard Garner (personal communication) has suggested this amplification: GO DIRECTLY TO ACTION, DO NOT PASS JUDGMENT, DO NOT COLLECT 200 OBLIGATIONS.
16. I do not mean to say that the determinism that governs human lives is all to be found at the "level" of belief/desire psychology. We are clearly ruled as well by less mentalist phenomena, such as habits. Thus, I intend all empirical assertions about motivation to be "all other things equal," and not only with respect to other beliefs and/or desires but also to things that are neither.
17. Even this might be going too far. See Steven Pinker's (1994, ch. 12) interesting discussion of "The Language Mavens."
18. Our insight into aesthetics, that is, the common concession that beauty is subjective, is remarkable, I think, given how powerfully we can be moved by art and music and natural beauty. I would be interested to read some empirical or reflective studies of why we are more able to maintain this distance or balance in aesthetics than in ethics. But accepting it as a fact that we are, I am therefore content that we retain "empirical aesthetics," that is, the language and feelings that are normally elicited by art and beauty. However, were the kind of heated arguments that are in fact quite common, such as whether a particular movie *is good* or who *is* the *greatest* composer or which style of art *is superior*, to become a basis of universal discord, rampant persecution, and armed conflict, then, because so much suffering were being caused by our mistaking something that is subjective for something that is objective, I might very well want to urge that we eliminate the aesthetic way of speaking that lent itself to this misuse. I suppose even that the phenomenon of *culture* could be understood as an attempt to create islands of faux objectivity in a subjective universe, for the illusion of objectivity is probably best preserved when everyone shares certain "tastes."

    By the way, another subjectivity that powerfully masquerades as objectivity is humor. I know that it is sometimes difficult (if not impossible) for me to believe that something I find exquisitely or hilariously funny is only so to me and folks of like sensibility but otherwise just is what it is, for example, some dialogue or slapstick routine. And would it not be very telling were somebody to become *seriously* bent out of shape because someone else did not share his sense that something was *funny*? (Ah, but what if he laughs at ethnic slurs and making children cry?)
19. I am also unconcerned to eliminate the language of "should" from talk about what is *rational*, but for the opposite reason (as also suggested in Chapter 2), namely, that I do not see any way to dispense with reason as a truly objective (even as it were metaphysical) standard. On the other hand, I can easily imagine someone *preferring* something else to rationality; for example, a person who in despair clings to the belief in an all-powerful and all-loving

Notes to Chapter 7   121

God in the face of extreme tragedy and horror. But this would only mean that, as always, I had no basis to *morally* judge this person, in this case, for being irrational. It would not mean that I could not judge the person to be irrational.

20. Note that I am *not* here speaking either about Sartre's ([1946] 1989) famous contention that we are "condemned to be free," or about so-called soft determinism, the doctrine that free will is compatible with, and in some formulations even dependent on our being causally determined. I am using "free" in the sense of being liberated from a burden, not of having a power to exercise self-control.
21. That is to say, for all practical purposes, i.e., putting aside quantum mechanical considerations.
22. I use "shall" as a kind of merger between "should" and "will" since, as I have been suggesting in effect, what you *should* do is what, other things equal, you *will* do once you have clarified your desires and beliefs. Meanwhile the personal pronoun "I" could be replaced by "we" for a group, even up to all competent human agents; but I avoid using the indefinite "one" since I do not want to suggest that the answer is expected to be the same for everyone. Thus, I am not only offering novel answers to the questions of ethics, but also novel questions.
23. In effect I am bringing Olympus down to sea level. In Plato's *Euthyphro* dialogue, the priest Euthyphro defines the pious thing to do as that which the gods love. Here "pious" is the translation of another merged notion (cf. the preceding note), this one combining divinity and morality; for Euthyphro and Socrates are discussing what is the right thing to do. Socrates famously refutes this definition in at least two ways, one of which is to point out its relativist implication (since different gods love different and sometimes conflicting things). What I have been arguing is that the ethical thing to do is what *people* "love," i.e., net-considered-desire; and, yes, this would lead to moral relativism if not for my also arguing that we should simply scrap morality and recognize our diversity of "loves" for what they are.
24. And thus another resolution of the notorious problem raised by Hume (1739, bk. 3, pt. 1., sec. 1) that deriving an *ought* from an *is* seems like getting blood from a stone: *Ought* (or *should*) is only a *hypothetical is*, viz., what you *would* do if. . . .
25. Indeed, if you think about it, the *giving up* of Santa Claus can be absolutely essential to achieving the purpose(s) Santa Claus serves; for if parents believed in Santa Claus, who would delight and reward the child with gifts?
26. This strikes me as exactly analogous to the manner in which evolutionary biology and cosmology have supplanted the need for a Creator God.
27. I am certain I have read advice similar to this—the impression is: regarding justice by a philosopher of emotion—but I have not been able to locate the source. When I first read it many years ago it left me cold; now I realize it left a lasting impression.
28. An old koan attributed to Zen Master Linji, founder of the Rinzai sect.
29. Aside from the rejection of evolution, the most bizarre feature to me of Christian pastor Rick Warren's argument in a debate he had with atheist Sam Harris (Meacham 2007) is its apparent egoism. Warren states, "If death is the end, shoot, I'm not going to waste another minute being altruistic." I would like to know why the suffering of another person or animal is not compelling enough in its own right to elicit our compassion and action. Why must there also be the carrot and stick? Do we really require nothing less than the prospect of eternal damnation or eternal bliss in order to be motivated to wipe the tears of a crying child?

Bibliography

American Dietetic Association. 2009. "Vegetarian Diets." *Journal of the American Dietetic Association* 109 (7): 1266–82.
Anscombe, G. E. M. 1958. "Modern Moral Philosophy." *Philosophy* 33 (124): 1–19.
Antony, Louise M., ed. 2007. *Philosophers without Gods: Meditations on Atheism and the Secular Life*. Oxford: Oxford University Press.
Aristotle. n.d. *Nicomachean Ethics*. Translated by W. D. Ross. http://classics.mit.edu/Aristotle/nicomachaen.html.
Armstrong, Karen. 1994. *A History of God*. New York: Ballantine Books.
Balcombe, Jonathan. 2006. *Pleasurable Kingdom: Animals and the Nature of Feeling Good*. New York: Macmillan.
Bekoff, Marc. 2007. *The Emotional Lives of Animals*. Novato, CA: New World Library.
Bekoff, Marc, and Jessica Pierce. 2009. *Wild Justice: The Moral Lives of Animals*. Chicago: University of Chicago Press.
(Pope) Benedict XVI. 2006. "Faith, Reason and the University: Memories and Reflections." Lecture at the University of Regensburg, September 12. http://www.vatican.va/holy_father/benedict_xvi/speeches/2006/september/documents/hf_ben-xvi_spe_20060912_university-regensburg_en.html.
Bergen, Peter. 2011. "A Long Time Going." *Time*, May 20, 44–45.
Best, Steven, and Anthony J. Nocella II, eds. 2004. *Terrorists or Freedom Fighters? Reflections on the Liberation of Animals*. New York: Lantern Books.
Boghossian, Paul. 2011. "The Maze of Moral Relativism." *Opinionator* (blog), *New York Times*, July 24. http://opinionator.blogs.nytimes.com/2011/07/24/the-maze-of-moral-relativism/.
Braithwaite, Victoria. 2010. *Do Fish Feel Pain?* Oxford: Oxford University Press.
Brandt, Richard B. 1979. *A Theory of the Good and the Right*. Oxford: Clarendon Press.
Broad, C. D. 1952. "Egoism as a Theory of Human Motives." In *Ethics and the History of Philosophy*, 218–31. London: Routledge and Kegan Paul.
Butler, (Bishop) Joseph. 1726. *Fifteen Sermons Preached at the Rolls Chapel*.
Carbone, Larry. 2004. *What Animals Want: Expertise and Advocacy in Laboratory Animal Welfare Policy*. Oxford: Oxford University Press.
Carruthers, Peter. 1992. *The Animals Issue: Moral Theory in Practice*. Cambridge: Cambridge University Press.
———. 1999. "Sympathy and Subjectivity." *Australasian Journal of Philosophy* 77: 465–82.
Cartwright, Nancy. 1999. *The Dappled World: A Study of the Boundaries of Science*. Cambridge: Cambridge University Press.

Ciocchetti, Christopher. 2012. "Veganism and Living Well." *Journal of Agricultural and Environmental Ethics* 25 (3): 405–17.
Clark, Tom. 2012. "How Can We Best Live, as Individuals and as a Society?" Naturalism.Org. http://www.naturalism.org/systematizing_naturalism.htm#ethics. Accessed April 9.
Cohon, Rachel. 2010. "Hume's Moral Philosophy." In *The Stanford Encyclopedia of Philosophy*, edited by Edward N. Zalta. http://plato.stanford.edu/archives/fall2010/entries/hume-moral/.
Cooney, Nick. 2011. *Change of Heart: What Psychology Can Teach Us about Spreading Social Change*. New York: Lantern Books.
Davis, Karen. 2009. *Prisoned Chickens, Poisoned Eggs: An Inside Look at the Modern Poultry Industry*. Revised edition. Summertown, TN: Book Publishing Co.
Dawkins, Richard. 2004. *The Ancestor's Tale: A Pilgrimage to the Dawn of Evolution*. Boston: Houghton Mifflin.
———. 2006. *The God Delusion*. Boston: Houghton Mifflin.
———. 2007. "Saddam Should Have Been Studied, Not Executed." *Los Angeles Times*, January 4.
Dennett, Daniel C. 1996. *Darwin's Dangerous Idea*. New York: Simon & Schuster.
———. 2006. *Breaking the Spell: Religion as a Natural Phenomenon*. New York: Penguin.
Diamond, Jared. 2002. "Evolution, Consequences and Future of Plant and Animal Domestication." *Nature* 418, August 8, 700–707.
Donagan, Alan. 1979. *The Theory of Morality*. Chicago: University of Chicago Press.
Douglas, Thomas. 2008. "Moral Enhancement." *Journal of Applied Philosophy* 25 (3): 228–45.
Drehle, David Von. 2011. "Death Comes for the Terrorist." *Time*, May 20, 16–28.
Dugger, Ronnie. 1984. "Does Reagan Expect a Nuclear Armageddon?" *Washington Post*, April 8, C1.
Engel, Mylan. 2000. "The Immorality of Eating Meat." In *The Moral Life*, edited by Louis P. Pojman, 856–89. New York: Oxford University Press.
Epstein, Greg. 2009. *Good without God: What a Billion Nonreligious People Do Believe*. New York: HarperCollins.
Feldman, Fred. 2006. "Actual Utility, the Objection from Impracticality, and the Move to Expected Utility." *Philosophical Studies* 129: 49–79.
Fetissenko, Maxim. 2011. "Beyond Morality: Developing a New Rhetorical Strategy for the Animal Rights Movement." *Journal of Animal Ethics* 1 (2): 150–75.
Fish, Stanley. 2011. "Does Philosophy Matter?" *Opinionator* (blog), *New York Times*, August 1. http://opinionator.blogs.nytimes.com/2011/08/01/does-philosophy-matter/.
Foot, Philippa. 1972. "Morality as a System of Hypothetical Imperatives." *Philosophical Review* 81 (3): 305–16.
———. 2001. *Natural Goodness*. Oxford: Clarendon.
Francione, Gary L. 2000. *An Introduction to Animal Rights: Your Child or the Dog?* Philadelphia: Temple University Press.
———. 2009. "A Revolution of the Heart." AbolitionistApproach.com, July 14. http://www.abolitionistapproach.com/a-revolution-of-the-heart/.
———. 2012. "Mission Statement." AbolitionistApproach.com. http://www.abolitionistapproach.com/about/mission-statement/. Accessed April 9.
Francione, Gary L., and Robert Garner. 2010. *The Animal Rights Debate: Abolition or Regulation?* New York: Columbia University Press.

Freud, Sigmund. 1927. *The Future of an Illusion.*
Garner, Richard. 1994. *Beyond Morality.* Philadelphia: Temple University Press.
———. 2011. "Morality: The Final Delusion?" *Philosophy Now* (82): 18–20.
Gendler, Tamar Szabó. 2008. "Alief and Belief." *Journal of Philosophy* 105 (10): 634–63.
Gilligan, Carol. 1982. *In a Different Voice: Psychological Theory and Women's Development.* Cambridge, MA: Harvard University Press.
Global Commission on Drug Policy. 2011. *War on Drugs.* http://www.globalcommissionondrugs.org/Report.
Green, O. Harvey. 1991. *The Emotions.* Dordrecht: Kluwer.
Greene, Joshua D. 2007. "The Secret Joke of Kant's Soul." In *The Neuroscience of Morality: Emotion, Disease, and Development*, edited by W. Sinnott-Armstrong. Cambridge, MA: MIT Press.
Greene, Joshua D., and Jonathan Cohen. 2004. "For the Law, Neuroscience Changes Nothing and Everything." *Philosophical Transactions of the Royal Society of London* B 359: 1775–85.
Hadley, John. 2009. "Animal Rights Extremism and the Terrorism Question." *Journal of Social Philosophy* 40 (3): 363–78.
Haidt, Jonathan. 2001. "The Emotional Dog and Its Rational Tail: A Social Intuitionist Approach to Moral Judgment." *Psychological Review* 108: 814–34.
Haidt, Jonathan, and Selin Kesebir. 2010. "Morality." In *Handbook of Social Psychology*, 5th ed., edited by S. Fiske, D. Gilbert, and G. Lindzey, 797–832. Hoboken, NJ: Wiley.
Hall, Lee. 2006. *Capers in the Churchyard: Animal Rights Advocacy in the Age of Terror.* Darien, CT: Nectar Bat Press.
———. 2010. *On Their Own Terms: Bringing Animal Rights Philosophy Down to Earth.* Darien, CT: Nectar Bat Press.
Harman, Gilbert H. 1965. "The Inference to the Best Explanation." *The Philosophical Review* 74 (1): 88–95.
Harris, Sam. 2010. *The Moral Landscape: How Science Can Determine Human Values.* New York: Free Press.
Hinckfuss, Ian. 1987. *The Moral Society—Its Structure and Effects.* Department of Philosophy, Research School of Social Sciences, Australian National University. http://www.uq.edu.au/~pdwgrey/web/morsoc/MoralSociety.pdf.
Hitchens, Christopher. 2007. *God Is Not Great: How Religion Poisons Everything.* New York: Twelve.
Humane Society of the United States. 2009. "Pet Overpopulation Estimates." HumaneSociety.org, November 23. http://www.humanesociety.org/issues/pet_overpopulation/facts/overpopulation_estimates.html.
Hume, David. 1739. *A Treatise of Human Nature.*
———. 1751. *An Enquiry Concerning the Principles of Morals.*
Ilea, Ramona. 2009. "Intensive Livestock Farming: Global Trends, Increased Environmental Concerns, and Ethical Solutions." *Journal of Agricultural and Environmental Ethics* 22 (2): 153–67.
Jacobson, Mark. 2010. *The Lampshade: A Holocaust Detective Story from Buchenwald to New Orleans.* New York: Simon & Schuster.
James, William. 1903. *The Varieties of Religious Experience.*
Joyce, Richard. 2001. *The Myth of Morality.* Cambridge: Cambridge University Press.
———. 2006. *The Evolution of Morality.* Cambridge, MA: MIT Press.
———. 2008. "Morality, Schmorality." In *Morality and Self-Interest*, edited by Paul Bloomfield, 51–75. Oxford: Oxford University Press.
———. 2011. "Moral Fictionalism." *Philosophy Now* (82): 14–17.

Bibliography

Kant, Immanuel. (1781) 1929. *Critique of Pure Reason*. Translated by Norman Kemp Smith. New York: St. Martin's.
———. (1785) 1993. *Groundwork of the Metaphysics of Morals*. Third edition. Translated by James W. Ellington. Indianapolis: Hackett.
———. 1795. *To Perpetual Peace*.
———. (1799) 1993. "On a Supposed Right to Lie Because of Philanthropic Concerns." In *Groundwork of the Metaphysics of Morals*, translated by James W. Ellington, 63–67. Indianapolis: Hackett.
Katz, David L. 2011. "E. Coli: Blame the Meat, Not the Sprouts." *Healthy Living* (blog), *Huffington Post*, June 6. http://www.huffingtonpost.com/david-katz-md/e-coli-vegetables-blame-meat_b_872055.html.
Kekes, John. 2011. "The Limits of Morality." Paper presented at a conference in honor of Joel Kupperman on Character: East and West, University of Connecticut at Storrs, May.
Kierkegaard, Søren. (1843) 1954. *Fear and Trembling*. Translated by Walter Lowrie. Princeton: Princeton University Press.
Knobe, Joshua. 2010. "Person as Scientist, Person as Moralist." *Behavioral and Brain Sciences* 33: 315–65.
Knobe, Joshua, and Shaun Nichols. 2008. "An Experimental Philosophy Manifesto." In *Experimental Philosophy*, edited by Joshua Knobe and Shaun Nichols. Oxford: Oxford University Press.
Kramer, Matthew. 2009. *Moral Realism as a Moral Doctrine*. Oxford: Wiley-Blackwell.
Krauss, Clifford. 2007. "Tyson Foods and ConocoPhillips to Produce Diesel Fuel from Animal Fat." *New York Times*, April 17.
Leibniz, G. W. 1710. *Théodicée* [Theodicy].
Lenman, James. 2000. "Consequentialism and Cluelessness." *Philosophy and Public Affairs* 29 (4): 342–70.
Linzey, Andrew. 2009. *Why Animal Suffering Matters*. Oxford: Oxford University Press.
Lurz, Robert W. 2002. "Reducing Consciousness by Making it Hot: A Review of Peter Carruthers' *Phenomenal Consciousness*." *Psyche* 8 (5). http://www.theassc.org/files/assc/2533.pdf.
Mackie, J. L. 1977. *Ethics: Inventing Right and Wrong*. London: Penguin.
MacKinnon, Catharine A. 2004. "Of Mice and Men: A Feminist Fragment on Animal Rights." In *Animal Rights: Current Debates and New Directions*, edited by Cass R. Sunstein and Martha C. Nussbaum, 263–76. Oxford: Oxford University Press.
Marks, Joel. 1982. "A Theory of Emotion." *Philosophical Studies* 42 (2): 227–42.
———. 1986a. "The Difference Between Motivation and Desire." In Marks, *The Ways of Desire*, 133–47.
———, ed. 1986b. *The Ways of Desire: New Essays in Philosophical Psychology on the Concept of Wanting*. Chicago: Precedent.
———. 1988. "When Is a Fallacy Not a Fallacy?" *Metaphilosophy* 19 (3 & 4): 307–12.
———. 2008. Review of *Capers in the Churchyard*, by Lee Hall. *Philosophy Now* (67): 43–45.
———. 2009. *Ought Implies Kant: A Reply to the Consequentialist Critique*. Lanham, MD: Lexington Books.
———. 2010a. "An Amoral Manifesto." *Philosophy Now* (80): 30–33 and (81): 23–26.
———. 2010b. "Innocent and Innocuous: The Case Against Animal Research." *Between the Species* 10: 98–117.
———. 2011. "Moral Pornography." *Philosophy Now* (87): 52.

Matthews, Christopher. 2006. "Livestock a Major Threat to Environment." *FAO Newsroom*, November 29. http://www.fao.org/newsroom/en/news/2006/1000448/index.html.
McLeod, Owen. 2001. "Just Plain 'Ought'." *The Journal of Ethics* 5 (4): 269–91.
McMahan, Jeff. 2008. "Eating Animals the Nice Way." *Daedalus* 137 (1): 66–76.
———. 2010. "The Meat Eaters." OntheHuman.org, September 18. http://onthehuman.org/2010/09/the-meat-eaters/.
Meacham, Jon. 2007. "God Debate: Sam Harris vs. Rick Warren." *Newsweek*, April 9.
Mellon, Margaret, C. Benbrook, and K. L. Benbrook. 2001. *Hogging It! Estimates of Antimicrobial Abuse in Livestock*. Cambridge, MA: Union of Concerned Scientists.
Mencius. *Mencius (Selections)*. Translated by Charles Muller. http://www.acmuller.net/con-dao/mencius.html.
Milgram, Stanley. 1974. *Obedience to Authority*. New York: Harper & Row.
Mill, John Stuart. 1861. *Utilitarianism*.
Mills, Charles W. 2011. "The Political Economy of Personhood." OntheHuman.org, April 4. http://onthehuman.org/2011/04/political-economy-of-personhood/.
Moeller, Hans-Georg. 2009. *The Moral Fool: A Case for Amorality*. New York: Columbia University Press.
Monk, Ray. 1990. *Ludwig Wittgenstein: The Duty of Genius*. New York: Free Press.
Montaigne, Michel de. 1580. *Les Essais* [Essays].
Mottershead, Clare. 2011. "The Unusual Uses for Animal Body Parts." BBC News Online, June 6. http://www.bbc.co.uk/news/science-environment-13670184.
Muir, John. (1911) 1998. *My First Summer in the Sierra*. New York: Houghton Mifflin.
Ozersky, Josh. 2011. "Carnist Challenge: Making Meat-Eating Cruelty-Free." Time.com, June 15. http://www.time.com/time/nation/article/0,8599,2077750,00.html?xid=fbshare.
Parfit, Derek. 1984. *Reasons and Persons*. Oxford: Clarendon.
The Pew Campaign on Human Health and Industrial Farming. 2012. http://www.saveantibiotics.org/ourwork.html. Accessed April 9.
Phelan, Mark. Forthcoming. "Experimental Philosophy: New Elephant on the Block." *Philosophy Now*.
Pigden, Charles. 1988. "Anscombe on 'Ought'." *Philosophical Quarterly* 38 (1): 20–41.
Pinker, Steven. 1994. *The Language Instinct*. New York: HarperCollins.
Pizarro, David. 2011. "Why Neuroscience Does Not Pose a Threat to Moral Responsibility." *AJOB Neuroscience* 2 (2): 1–2.
Plato. 1981. *Euthyphro*. In *Five Dialogues*. Translated by G. M. A. Grube. Indianapolis: Hackett.
———. 2001. *Phaedo*. Translated by Benjamin Jowett. www.bartleby.com/2/1/.
Posner, Richard A., and Peter Singer. 2001. "Animal Rights." Slate.com, June 12. http://www.slate.com/articles/news_and_politics/dialogues/features/2001/animal_rights/_2.html.
Prinz, Jesse. 2007. *The Emotional Construction of Morals*. Oxford: Oxford University Press.
Regan, Tom. 2004. "How to Justify Violence." In Best and Nocella, *Terrorists or Freedom Fighters?* 231–36.
Rossi, Philip. 2009. "Kant's Philosophy of Religion." In *The Stanford Encyclopedia of Philosophy*, edited by Edward N. Zalta. <http://plato.stanford.edu/archives/win2009/entries/kant-religion/>.
Sarkissian, H., J. Park, D. Tien, J. C. Wright, and J. Knobe. 2011. "Folk Moral Relativism." *Mind & Language* 26: 482–505.

Bibliography

Sartre, Jean Paul. (1943) 1956. *Being and Nothingness*. Translated by Hazel E. Barnes. New York: Washington Square Press.

———. (1946) 1989. "Existentialism Is a Humanism." Translated by Philip Mairet. In *Existentialism from Dostoyevsky to Sartre*, edited by Walter Kaufmann, 287–311. New York: Meridian.

Schroeder, Timothy. 2004. *Three Faces of Desire*. Oxford: Oxford University Press.

Scruton, Roger. 2006. "Eating Our Friends." In *A Political Philosophy: Arguments for Conservatism*, 47–63. London: Continuum.

Silver, Mitchell. 2006. *A Plausible God: Secular Reflections on Liberal Jewish Theology*. New York: Fordham University Press.

———. 2011. "Our Morality: A Defense of Moral Objectivism." *Philosophy Now* (83): 21–24.

Singer, Peter. 1975. *Animal Liberation*. New York: Random House.

Singer, Peter, and Jim Mason. 2006. *The Way We Eat: Why Our Food Choices Matter*. N.p.: Rodale.

Smith, Huston. 1965. *The Religions of Man*. New York: Harper & Row.

Statman, Daniel, ed. 1993. *Moral Luck*. Albany: State University of New York Press.

Steiner, Gary. 2009. "Animal, Vegetable, Miserable." *New York Times*, November 22.

Stich, Stephen P. 1983. *From Folk Psychology to Cognitive Science: The Case Against Belief*. Cambridge, MA: MIT Press.

———. 2008. "Some Questions About *The Evolution of Morality*." *Philosophy and Phenomenological Research* 77 (1): 228–36.

Strawson, P. F. 1963. *Individuals: An Essay in Descriptive Metaphysics*. Garden City, NY: Anchor Books.

Wong, David. 2006. *Natural Moralities: A Defense of Pluralistic Relativism*. New York: Oxford University Press.

———. 2011. "Making the Effort to Understand." *Philosophy Now* (82): 10–13.

Wood, Allen. Forthcoming. "Kant on Conscience." *Kantovski Sbornik*.

Yeates, James W. 2010. "Death Is a Welfare Issue." *Journal of Agricultural and Environmental Ethics* 23: 229–41.

Zakaria, Fareed. 2011. "When Terror Loses Its Grip." *Time*, May 20, 50–51.

Zimmerman, M. 1962. "The 'Is-Ought': An Unnecessary Dualism." *Mind*, New Series 71 (281): 53–61.

Index

A
abolitionism, animal, 68–81, 113n9, 113n14
abolitionism, moral, 104n4, 109n2
abortion, 47, 75
activism. *See* animal ethics
aesthetics, 90, 119n10, 120n18
akrasia. *See* weakness of will
alief, 108n38
amoralism, basic vs. full-blown, 26, 99n1. *See also* deism, moral
amorality (full-blown amoralism), xi
   advantages of, 32–33, 35–55, 87–90
   as practicable, 62–63
   as self-refuting, 82
   criterion of, 53
   equivalence of, to morality, 56–63
   losses attendant on, 35, 92
   qualities of, I like, 48–55
   transition costs of, 109n53
   viability of, 26–34, 37–38
   See also abolitionism, moral; ethics, amoral
anger, xiii, 40–42, 51
animal activism. *See* animal ethics
animal advocacy. *See* animal ethics
animal ethics, 67–81, 107n29
   amoralist approach to, 72–73, 78–81
animals
   experimentation on, 115n35
   use of, for food. *See* factory farming
Anscombe, G. E. M., 107n34
antibiotics, 117n60
antidisestablishmentarianism, 49
anti-realism, moral, 104n4
Antony, Louise M., 3
Apes, Beneath the Planet of the (movie), 116n37
Armstrong, Karen, 109n1
atheism, 109n1
   relation of, to amorality, xi, 3, 99n3.
   See also hard atheism
   See also God
autonomy, 70–71

B
baby
   throwing out the, but keeping the bath water, 111n24
   throwing out the, with the bath water, 65–66, 91
bad faith, 114n31
Bad Faith (memoir), ix-xii, xiv, 54, 92, 105n12, 106n21
Beautiful Mind, A (movie), 118n3
Bekoff, Marc, 114n24, 116n46, 119n7
belief
   as fallible, 60, 111n17
   as motivating, 102n11
(Pope) Benedict XVI, 46–47
best explanation, inference to the, 16–25, 61, 83–85, 107n36
Bigfoot, 9
bin Laden, Osama, 50, 54, 75, 107n36
Boghossian, Paul, 111n18
Brandt, Richard B., 118n61
Buddha, 71–72, 93
Buddha nature, 53–54

C
Carbone, Larry, 114n25, 117n52
Carruthers, Peter, 112n5
categorical imperative
   as normative, 12–13
   as meta-ethical, 13–15, 86–87
cause and effect, 74, 119n7. *See also* determinism; explanation
childishness, 114n31

child rearing, 93
church and state, 49
circumcision, female, 60–61
Clark, Tom, 110n9
cognitive psychotherapy, 118n61
Cohon, Rachel, 110n14
compassion, 53–54, 91–93
conformism, 76–77
consent, 70, 114n25
constructivism
  amoral, 59
  moral, 58–59
contingency, 91
counter-conversion, 27
culture, 120n18

D

Darwinism. *See* evolution
Davis, Karen, 116n46, 117n52
death penalty, 43, 108n41
decision making. *See* practical reason
deism, moral, 104n4
Delphic injunction, 108n44
democracy, 47, 111n26
description, morally neutral, 83
desert, moral, 52, 104n2
desirable (the word), 106n25
desire, 46
  acting contrary to, 27–28
  as basis of value, 36, 38
  brute, 119n7
  distinctions of, 27, 28
  intentional object vs. cause of, 106n18
  See also moral desire
desirism, 27–28, 38, 57, 90–91
  difference of, from egoism, 31–32
  See also amorality, criterion of
determinism, 41–42, 90–91, 102n6, 120n16. *See also* will, free
Diamond, Jared, 117n57
drugs. *See* War on Drugs
drunken driver, 52
dualism, 22–23, 84–85

E

egoism, 31–32
egotism, 42–43
emotions. *See* feelings; reason vs. emotion
empathy, 89
empirical morality, 17
  conflation of, with conceptual morality, 64

Engel, Mylan, 117n54
environmental ethics, 69, 79
epistemology, 18–19, 22, 65, 84–85
error theory, moral, 104n4
ethics
  amoral, 85–91
  as hypothetical, 86–87
  as motivating, 89–91
  maxim of, 86
  practicality of, 46, 87–90
  similarity of normative, to theology, 46–47
  types of, 10–11
Euthyphro (Platonic dialogue), 19, 100n16, 106n27, 107n30, 121n23
evolution, 17, 18, 25, 31, 57–58, 84, 119n4
experimental philosophy, 16, 56, 96n6, 99n6, 102n8
explanation vs. justification, 83–85
exploitation. *See* use

F

factory farming, 67, 74–75, 117n60
facts (considerations). *See* feelings and facts
fairness, 83, 87–89, 92
feelings, 40, 74–77, 92, 106n24, 118n3
  and facts, 53, 107n29. *See also* empathy
feminist ethics, 69
Fetissenko, Maxim, 113n13, 117n53
fictionalism, moral, 62–63, 99n1
  amoral variant of, 104n4
Fish, Stanley, 104n1
folk psychology, 97n25
Foot, Philippa, 97n20, 97n23, 101n36, 114n31, 119n8
Francione, Gary L., 118n62, 118n65
free will. *See* will
functionalism, moral, 60, 62

G

Garner, Richard, xii-xiii, 108n37, 108n46, 109n2, 111n23, 120n15
Garner, Robert, 113n20
Gendler, Tamar Szabó, 108n38
global warming, 79
God
  and egotism, 44
  and the explanation of morality, 18, 19–21, 59

similarity of, to morality, ix-x, 5, 16, 46, 109n5
See also atheism
grammar, 90
Green, O. Harvey, 107n28
guilt, moral, 48

H

habit, 120n16
Haidt, Jonathan, 109n2, 109n6, 110n8
Hall, Lee, 113nn9-10, 114n27, 114n29, 115n36, 116n39, 118n62
hard atheism, 20-21. *See also* atheism
hard moralism, 109n52
Heston, Charlton, 116n37
Hinckfuss, Ian, 96n6, 106n22
history, 39-40
Hitler, Adolf, 39-41
humane treatment. *See* use
Humeanism, 58-59
humor, 120n18
hypocrisy, 42, 105n16
hypotheticalness (of ethics), 86-87, 90

I

ideals, ethical, 29, 41, 73, 92-93
 and moral values, 32-33
Ignoble Lie, 104n4
Ilea, Ramona, 117n56
illusions, 82, 92
indignation, 41
intuition, xiii-xiv, 21, 57-58, 76, 77-78, 84-85, 118n3

J

jaywalkers, braking for, 51, 53
Joe Friday, 53
Joyce, Richard, xiv, 101n35, 111nn21-22, 119n11. *See also* fictionalism, moral
"just" (as in "I just don't like it"), 119n7
justification, moral, 83-85

K

Kantianism, 23, 100n18, 100n26
 as an ethical ideal (vs. a moral imperative), 32, 103n14
 See also categorical imperative as normative; Kingdom of Ends
Katz, David, 117n58
Kekes, John, 106n26, 111n29, 119n10

Kingdom of Ends, 21-23
Knobe, Joshua, 101n32
knowledge. *See* epistemology
Koepsell, David, 108n39

L

law. *See* morality as lawlike
Leibniz, G. W., 24
Linzey, Andrew, 113n7
luck, moral, 52
Lycan, William, 102n11
lying, 23, 24-25, 60, 105n16

M

Mack, Ron, 106n24
Matrix, The (movie), 116n38
maxim, 86
McLeod, Owen, 96n15
McMahan, Jeff, 113n18, 114n27
meditation, yogic, 53
memoir. *See Bad Faith*
Mencius, 114n31
meta-ethics, 10, 15
 practical import of, 104n1
metaphysical morality, 17, 20-22, 25, 84-85, 92
"Might makes right," 10
Milgram, Stanley, 43
misanthropy, 76, 116n39
Moeller, Hans-Georg, 103n19, 106n22
Monk, Ray, 95nn6-7, 97n24
monotheorism, 11
Montaigne, Michel de, 58
moral (the word), ambiguity of, 6, 46, 65, 97n19
moral concepts, inventory of, 52
moral desire, 27, 29, 58
moralism (the word), ambiguity of, 111n28
morality
 and circumstances, 111n16
 and practical reason, 6-9
 and value, 36-37
 as adaptive (providing selective advantage), 31
 as arbitrary, 44
 as categorical, 13-15
 as a delusion, 118n3
 as a human institution, 1, 16. *See also* empirical morality
 as a manifold concept, 9-13
 as an incoherent concept, 10, 20-21
 as a type of value, 97n28
 as dangerous, 66, 106n22

as functional. *See* functionalism, moral
as ineffectual, 30, 72, 74, 85–86, 113n13
as lawlike, 4–5, 16, 102n11
as monotypic, 11
as non-existent, 1, 16
as overriding, 6, 44
as redundant, 28–30
as relative. *See* relativism, moral
as secular, 5
as uncompromising, 45
as useless or worse than useless. *See* morality as ineffectual
authority of, 57, 58, 59, 61, 62, 63. *See also* morality as categorical
conflation of, with moralizing, 63–65
essence of, 91–92
explanation of. *See* inference to the best explanation
inescapability of, 82
my conception of, 4–15. *See also* metaphysical morality
qualities of, I don't like, 40–48
reforming the concept of, 11, 56–57, 62, 109n2
relation of, to God. *See* God
relation of, to religion. *See* religion
schizophrenic view of, by moral psychologists and philosophers, 61, 109n6
types of, vs. as such, 10–11
moralizing, 63–65
moral masochism, 107n32
moral pornography, 105n15
moral relativism. *See* relativism, moral
moreality, 1

N
Nash, John, 118n3
naturalism, moral, 57–58
Nazi Germany, 76–77
new atheists. *See* atheism
Nietzsche, Friedrich, 105n12
Noble Lie, 26, 31, 64
  reverse of, 104n4

O
Obama, Barack, 50, 107n36
objective elements of ethics, 103n14
objective value, 36
  egotism and, 44

objectivity, faux, 120n18
Occam's razor, 18–19
ought (moral obligation)
  deriving, from is (nonmoral reality), 110n14, 121n24
  deriving is from, 89–91
ought (the word), dispensability of, 90–91
Ozersky, Josh, 118n67

P
Peaceable Kingdom (movie), 116n47
permissibility, 96n16
person (concept) as inherently moral, 24–25
persons
  as inherently valuable, 36–37
  as morally considerable, 35, 91
pets, 67–68, 70–71, 75
Phelan, Mark, 102n8
philomoralia, 42
philosophy
  and introspection, 105n10
  as a profession, 107n31
  as subjective, 2, 41, 105n12
  two methods of, 2–3
Pizarro, David, 119n4
plagues, 79
Posner, Richard A., 107n29
predator and prey animals, 114n27
prediction in lieu of prescription, 91
principle, standing on, 42, 44–45
Prinz, Jesse, 105n9
psychology, folk, 97n25

R
rationality, 120n19
reason, practical
  and ethics, 119n12
  and morality, 6–9, 23
  as prudential, 7–8
  vs. emotion, 111n25
  vs. rationalizing, 64, 65
red pill, 116n38
reform, moral, 58
reforming definition. *See* morality, reforming the concept of
Regan, Tom, 115n35
relativism, moral, x, 47, 59–62
  equivalence of, to amorality, xi
religion
  and guilt, 48–49
  and intolerance, 49
  See also God

respect
    for animals (sentient beings, human and nonhuman), 69–70, 91
    for persons, 98n42. *See also* categorical imperative as normative
rights, animal, 69–71, 114n22
rights, moral, 35, 45

S

Santa Claus, 1, 21, 25, 53, 92, 121n25
Sartre, Jean Paul, 102n11
schmorality, 87, 119n11
Scruton, Roger, 118n64
self-image, 29, 73, 92–93
sentience, 113n21
shall (the word), 121n22
sheep and goats, parable of, 107n33
Sherlock Holmes, 10, 38
shock (presumed medical condition), 10
should (the word). *See* ought (the word)
Silver, Mitchell, xiii-xiv, 109n5, 119n10
sin, 16, 48–49
Singer, Peter, 107n29, 112n2, 117n52
Socrates, 107n31. *See also* Euthyphro
solipsism, 91
soylent green, 79
speciesism, 77–78
    as moralist, 116n41
Steiner, Gary, 114n30
stepfather, 87–89
Stich, Stephen P., 97n25
stick in water, bent (illusion), 82
stories as explanations, 21–23
straw person, attacking a, 63–65
stubborn moralism, 119n4
subjectivity, 2, 36, 41, 103n14, 111n20

T

tar baby, 72
telos, the highest. *See* morality as overriding

tipping (a waiter), 45
tolerance, 49–50
transhumanism, 119n4
truth, value of, 35, 38, 54–55
tu quoque, 43, 82

U

unicorns, 56–57
use vs. abuse, 67–70, 114n30
utilitarianism, 13, 32–33, 70

V

value, 35–36, 97n28
    inherent, 69–71
        vs. intrinsic, 36–37
        vs. preference, 116n41
veganism, 74, 75, 80, 114n30, 115n32
Vegan Outreach, 117n50
vegetarianism, 114n31, 115n33, 117n59. *See also* veganism
violence, 53, 72–73, 74–78

W

Wallach, Wendell, xiv
War on Drugs, 66
Warren, Rick, 121n29
weakness of will, 30, 74, 89, 102n11
Weiner, Anthony, 105n16
welfare, animal, 68–71, 113nn20–21
Wheeler III, Samuel C., 111n17
will, free, 4–5, 22, 27–28, 50, 107n36
    freedom from, 91
    See also weakness of will
witches, 3, 17, 97n31
Wittgenstein, Ludwig, 95nn6–7
worth. *See* value
wounded man, parable of the, 71–72

Y

Yeates, James W., 112n6

Z

Zimmerman, M., 108n46